LEAVE A FOOTPRINT

CHANGE THE WHOLE WORLD

TIM BAKER

ZONDERVAN®

ZONDERVAN.com/
AUTHORTRACKER
follow your favorite authors

ZONDERVAN®

Leave a Footprint—Change the Whole World
Copyright © 2009 by Tim Baker

Requests for information should be addressed to:
Zondervan, *Grand Rapids, Michigan* 49530

ISBN 978-0-310-27885-6

International Trade Paper Edition

Cover design by SharpSeven Design
Interior design by Brandi Etheredge Design

Printed in the United States of America

09 10 11 12 13 14 • 23 22 21 20 19 18 17 16 15 14 13 12 11 10 9 8 7 6 5 4 3 2

For Ruth Shorey...
Teacher. Missionary. Mother. Wife. Life-shaping friend to hundreds of people. You effortlessly lived the love of Jesus, traveling the world with joy and color, enthusiastically seeking to bring others to the Savior you loved so dearly. The world felt heavier when you left it. We miss you.

ACKNOWLEDGMENTS

Thanks to the people who worked hard to pull this book together, and who provided encouragement along the way...

Jay Howver and everyone at the YS publishing team. You are good people doing good work. Thanks for the gift of working with you.

Doug Davidson. You're the biggest prize any author has ever received. Where have you been all my life? Thanks for your unending patience, for making dozens of changes, and for challenging me.

My church family at Hope Fellowship. Your encouragement through the writing of this book means the world to me. Ben, somewhere along the way in this project you stopped being senior pastor and became my very good friend. What a good friend you are.

Nicole, Jessica, and Jacob Baker. Travel. Learn. Be grace-filled. Seek forgiveness, peace, and reconciliation. Keep your eyes fixed on the horizon. Don't settle for stale, prepackaged answers. Love everyone you meet. Thanks for being God's young hands in my life.

And Jacqui. You make our marriage a poetic praise to God. You've sacrificed more than anyone could know so I could write this book. I love you.

CONTENTS

chapter 1

WHAT IF YOU COULD WALK
THE PLANET BAREFOOT...
...would others want to follow your tracks?

Small, very-used-up toys and old baby pushcarts often litter our church's small nursery. As on most other Sunday mornings, there were a few toddlers struggling to move around on the floor, their attentions shifting quickly from one toy to another. Julie sat in the room rocking babies, building red and yellow block castles, and changing an occasional diaper.

I'd met Julie four years earlier, when she was a freshman in college, and we'd been friends since. Julie had always seemed wise well beyond her years—an old soul trapped in her young body. She was quiet, but not timid, and often spoke with restrained strength. And there was always laughter flowing out of her. You know how it is when you have a friend who's about to graduate or move? It seems like the last few conversations you have with these friends are always the best ones...the ones that make you say to yourself and to them how much you wish they weren't moving away because you want to have more good talks—even though you really haven't had that many really great talks. Well, as I sat in the nursery with Julie that day, that's the kind of talking we did. Julie's graduation was rocketing toward her, and she was stressing...feeling unready to go out into the world. It was too much pressure. Julie was caving...

And drowning...

And worrying...

She'd been studying to be an airplane mechanic, but as graduation approached she was questioning the decision she'd made years earlier. Did she really believe God had led her to this major? Had she made the right decision investing four years of her life at this university? Should she have become a pilot? An English teacher? A politician? She'd loved airplanes since she was a kid, but doubt was creeping in and ruining the certainty she'd had about her future, and stress was taking over and making her feel like she'd chosen the wrong major. After investing a lot of time, money, and emotion imagining herself as the jumpsuit-wearing airplane-mechanic girl, she was realizing now that airplanes were the last occupation on her list.

And, it felt like everyone had gotten in the disappointment line, waiting to blast her for any change in major or life direction. People like...

Her parents... They'd spent tons of money sending her to the "right" school. They'd invested countless hours on the phone encouraging her. They'd shared their pride in her to their friends. Their focus was on Julie actually doing what she'd been training to do.

Her friends... They were all heading off to do what they'd been preparing four years to start doing. Grad school. Their first jobs. Getting married. Buying a car...renting a house...finding new places to hang out.

Her teachers... They'd invested hours teaching her the finer points of overhauling airplane engines. Her advisor had spent more than a lot of time working with her to craft the right course schedules.

And Julie, herself... She was afraid she was ruining her entire future and life. She didn't want to let anyone down, including God. It was a weighty time for her.

How do you take on the world when you're not sure you're really ready—and not sure you really want to do what you've been saying you want to do for years? How do you live with the tension of doing what God wants, what your parents expect, and what you love? How can you know God's will for your life so clearly that you don't mess up what he wants you to do?

A DIVINE BLUEPRINT?

I tried. I did my best to ease Julie's fears. I'm sure you know how compassion kicks in when you see a friend hurting. It spills out of you like warm hot chocolate. I offered her my sweet warm fuzzy ideas... "God loves you no matter what," I said. "You'll be fine, just take a step of faith, and make sure you honor God with what occupation you do choose," I continued.

I'm not convinced I helped Julie much. That's probably because I'm not sure I'm convinced about the whole "God's will" scenario Christians often toss around. I'm not sure I believe God has some kind of pre-ordained overarching plan for our entire lives. I'm not sure I grasp God's will as a preprogrammed, shrink-wrapped, and packaged-up idea God makes for each and every believer.

Ever since I was a kid, I've admired my dad's occupation. He was a civil engineer—the guy you'd call on if you wanted to build a building that didn't fall down. Dad would take me to his office and I'd see the long, flat drawers lining the walls. And in those drawers were large blueprints that smelled like old blue ink. I'd walk in, pull myself up onto one of the tall chairs that lined his blueprint table, and look over whatever plans my dad was working on, trying to understand what all the lines and marks and notes meant. I never could grasp what they said, because reading a blueprint for a building is both an art and a science. You need both sides of your brain working at the same time.

The planning and forward-thinking it takes to create a building astounds me. An architect has to envision every corner, every nook, every wall, and much more, giving careful thought to where wires, conduits, air ducts, closets, and all that other stuff will go. All of that goes on the blueprint. All of it is figured out before the first shovel hits the earth.

My dad's trained mind and keen eye were monumental things to me. He was a building magician, able to put these structures together, organize the people needed, get the money required, stay on schedule, get deliveries on time, hold meetings, plan openings, look for finishing touches, and—probably the most difficult aspect of all of that—work with the myriad of problems that come up during the building process.

Several years ago, when I was at a very crucial point in my development as a believer, I was calling out to God and asking him for direction. I wanted God to tell me what I was supposed to do for him. *"Please show me your will"* I would pray. *"Maybe God, if I could just see the bigger picture of my life."* And if I lacked faith or hadn't heard anything, I'd desperately cry out, *"Just show me my next step!"* I'd make sure God knew I'd give him the praise for anything good that happened in my life as a result of obeying his plan. I'd invite people to see the glory of God pronounced undeniably in the beautiful building of the life he designed for me. And, should any of that fall apart—if anything bad happened as a result of my following God's plan—then I'd take the blame. It'd be my fault because bad and uncomfortable or unsuccessful things only happen to weak believers or, worse, disobedient believers. And, should something monumentally awesome happen—maybe I win a million dollars following God's plan, or I get the chance to speak at a presidential election ceremony, or I get my face on a cereal box—then God would certainly get that praise, too. I'd praise him on the drive over to the bank where I'd deposit that huge check you get following God's perfect plan.

Somehow, in the cosmic weirdness of my mind, I made God out to be a supercharged version of my dad. God was the guy in heaven making blueprints of my life, taking them out whenever I had a question about what direction or next step to take, reviewing them, looking over what he'd planned out, then letting me know what I was supposed to do next. Ever wonder what God does all day? Well, I imagined him spending every moment looking over his perfectly crafted, predetermined, unchangeable plans and letting us know what we're supposed to do with ourselves here on planet Earth. He'd look over them as architect, engineer, and artist, seeing our glorious end, our financial prosperity, our emotional wholeness, and our occupational success. And as he looked them over, he'd wring his hands and say to himself, "If only they'll be obedient robots and do what I programmed them to do. If only they'll be holy enough so I can tell them what I want them to do with their lives." At least that's what I thought.

When you believe God has everything in your life pre-planned like a blueprint, you view everything that happens to you as part of that blueprint. I now realize that when I would pray those things— like, "Please show me your will" and "Help me see the big picture" and "Just show me my next step"—I was actually taking away from the beauty of how God created me. I was no longer unique or special. My life could not ebb and flow. I could not go through moments of doubt or joy. I was saying to God, "Please, God, help me be more like the robot you created me to be." If I wanted to be God's good robot, I could not depart from his plan which was somehow built into me as a part of my soul. And in my thinking, the way for me to really tap into that plan was to pray. A lot. The way to know the plan of God for me was unending prayer, fasting, Bible reading, and worship. Slowly, one day at a time, if I was being obedient enough and praying enough and seeking enough, God would reveal his plan, the plan already built into me. I would just know it. It would be an open door. I'd walk through, I'd be there, and I'd be content.

I had excuses for God and me if I never deciphered the plan. If I couldn't figure it out, I wasn't praying enough. If it seemed too big, I lacked faith. If I only knew one right decision to make, God was letting me know one little bit at a time—letting me know only so much because if I knew everything I'd run and hide in the closet like a scared kid.

And, if I ever doubted my whole idea of blueprint living, I had Scriptures that seemed to back up the idea—Scriptures like this one:

Your eyes saw my unformed body. All the days ordained for me were written in your book before one of them came to be. (Psalm 139:16)

When I read that "the days ordained for me" were written in God's book, I imagined my life as a story that had already been written. God knew the plot, the number of pages, and all the characters—and none of those could change. So I'd devote myself to asking God what was in the next chapter. I'd dump *seeing*, *knowing*, and *determining* into the same bucket, call them the same thing, and believe that God's knowing me from before my birth meant he directed every second of *The Me Show*.

Or, there was this verse...

"For I know the plans I have for you," declares the Lord, "plans to prosper you and not to harm you, plans to give you hope and a future." (Jeremiah 29:11)

I would forget those words were written to captive Israel, and not to non-captive me. I'd read "plans I have for you" and imagine God had specific plans that never changed, that they were always good and included no pain, poverty, uncertainty, questioning, or times when God feels silent, even though Israel experienced all of those.

Or this verse...

Do not conform any longer to the pattern of this world, but be transformed by the renewing of your mind. Then you will be able to test and approve what God's will is—his good, pleasing and perfect will. (Romans 12:2)

I'd ignore context here, too, and imagine the good, pleasing, and perfect will of God that Paul spoke of was a predetermined plan, and the more I sacrificed myself, the more I'd know about that will.

The reverse of that is obvious, isn't it? If I didn't know God's will, then there was something wrong with my walk with God. Think that through...holy, spiritually perfect people know God's will. The rest of us, those who are honestly pursuing God yet don't have his plans for us all figured out, are unholy.

Those passages were just enough Scripture to make me think there was some divine blueprint called *God's Will for Your Life*, but not enough to give me the path to how I could ever know what that will was. They led me to years of searching for a hand from the sky that would show me God's will.

THE WRONG QUESTIONS?

So when I talked to Julie that day in the church nursery, I understood what she was looking for. It's the same thing I've been looking for when I've asked those questions. And I bet it's the same quest you've been on, too. We want to know God's will for us, *for certain*. We want to know *for sure* that what we're doing with our lives, or what we've committed to doing, is exactly what God wants us to do. We want the exact plan and we don't want to wait for it. We don't want the future to be muddy. We want the certainty of the good soldier who's got the commander's orders tucked away in his pocket. Those orders need to be specific, measurable, detailed, and stamped with the seal of our commander, God—the giver of all orders for his army.

But is that the personality of God? Is he the blueprint-making, plan-scheming, order-giving guy who determines our every step? Does he keep his plans from us until we've been good enough, prayed enough, devoted ourselves enough? Does he wait until we are ready for his will, and then bestow it on us like a prize? Is the discovery of his will the result of hours of hard work?

I don't really think God wants us to come to him and ask to see the blueprint. Instead, I think he wants each of us to say, "Lead me into that next step." We want certainty, but God wants us to stay uncertain. He wants to direct our next step, not show us a detailed plan for our entire lives. Maybe that's because God knows we're not ready to know the whole story. Maybe God just wants our every step to be rooted in dependence on him. Maybe he doesn't tell us more than we need to know, because if we could see all that's ahead of us, we might be so scared we'd never move.

The myth of God as the all-knowing blueprint-hiding guy in the sky has served us well. We've needed to see him as that kind of God during those times when we're not clear on what we're supposed to do with our lives. And, I think we've needed God to be that kind of guy, because...

We're reluctant to admit we don't really know what God's will is.
There's a reason why you'll get 17 different answers if you ask six people what God's will is for you and how you're supposed to find it. Humans created the theory that we can easily discover God's will because it helps us feel better about what we're doing with our lives. If there's a blueprint labeled "God's will" that governs everything that happens in our lives, then we don't have to think about our own direction. We aren't responsible for our own decisions. We don't have to concentrate too hard on where we're going in life, because everything we do is part of God's overarching will for us. Every single thing that happens to us—positive or negative—is the result of God's predetermined, unchangeable will.

We're more comfortable waiting than doing.
It's also common for "God's will" to be offered as an excuse for making mistakes or not doing anything. We encourage people to wait for God's will, spend time seeking God's will, and in doing that, we don't really have to do anything...just wait. The longer we wait, the holier we seem once we've "heard" God.

But what makes Christianity so special that those of us who follow Jesus get to sit around and wait until we hear something from

God? How many people have you met who've seemed more spiritual when they've finally "heard God's call"? Why do we get to do nothing until we hear something?

"God's will" can explain why things don't go as we'd planned.
Suppose a believer gets in over her head in a job—the position is too much, and she doesn't rise to the challenge. She struggles with her responsibilities, things get mixed up, and she gets fired. Once the firing happens, the words come quickly...the position wasn't what God had in mind for her. It was outside God's will. He didn't want it for her, so he arranged it so the job didn't work out. But what if God wanted her in that position, and she totally blew it? What if God's will was that she remain in that position for as long as she could possibly stay? What if she was God's person for the job...but then she messed things up and mucked up the divine plan?

The more I read the Bible, and the more I listen to people talk about what they think God's will is, the more I'm convinced that we're imposing our ideas about God's will on God rather than building our understanding on what we find in God's Word. We want so badly for God to have an exact call and will for us that we create the idea that he has a specific will for us. Then, we create steps about finding God's will that don't exist in the Bible.

Can I offer an alternate idea? What if we understood God as the one who lovingly created us and continues to shape us into the people he longs for us to be? What if we understand God as the loving parent who imagines what we'll be like before we're born, who wrings his hands awaiting our birth, and then watches us grow into the wonderful people he imagined? And what if, in all of that, we understood God's desire was not that each of us would follow some pre-designed path like a rat in a maze, but instead that we would all lovingly live out our lives in response to the wonder and imagination with which we were created? If we did that, we'd discover the truth of God's will, that it isn't some blueprint we have to follow, but something we live in response to who God created us to be. We'd fall in love with God all over again, and instead of spending all our energy to figure out God's plan, we'd start living lives of meaning and passion in response to God's love.

SANDY FOOTPRINTS

The New Testament is full of stories of people who live this way. Paul willingly followed wherever God led. Peter was always willing to confront and travel and lead the early church. Luke, who traveled with Paul for at least a few journeys, was obviously willing to search out the truths of Christ and follow what truth he uncovered. But we never read of Paul, a tentmaker by trade, praying and asking for God's will for making tents. Peter, a fisherman, never says anything recorded about God's specific plan for him as a fisherman. And Luke, a doctor who willingly followed God's direction, never seems interested in knowing God's will about what kind of medicine he's called to practice, or where he should open a clinic. Should he heal people in Macedonia? Should he open a practice in Jerusalem? Luke never says. Paul and Peter don't, either.

These people weren't looking for a specific plan called "God's will" for their entire lives or occupations. Their focus on the will of God, the direction and plan of God, was a truth-spreading, salt-living focus. They were interested in making an impact for Christ on the planet, not waiting around, praying hard but barely moving, obediently pacifying themselves with a measly occupation until they heard Holy Spirit magic from heaven. They were active. They were working. They were striving to help others or they were striving toward being like Christ, passionate about being God's people—how he created them to be and who he created them to be—and they were living that out passionately. As I read the New Testament, that is God's total will for them—to love others, to serve God, and to live passionately the way they were created to live.

These people walked the planet with the message of God, living in ways that glorified him. Like people walking barefoot on a beach, these first followers of Christ left a footprint with every step. Their lives made a mark. Their actions touched the souls of those they encountered. And the truth of God's Word in them, the shape of their feet, the number of their toes, was left behind in little gatherings of believers, in families, on the hearts of men and women. Their footprints are left in the sand for us to see and to marvel at the determined path walked by each one.

When I watch people graduate from high school or college, I wonder, what footprints will they leave? What path will they ultimately take? Where will they invest themselves? Will they ever really change the world? I wonder if they see the potential they have within them to do mighty, footprint-leaving, world-denting things. Most often, I see students with a bucket full of stuff (textbooks, a major, some fun ideas, debt) but with no real direction—just a hope that they'll find something to occupy themselves until they die, or until they ultimately discover a purpose. I see people easily distracted by sandcastles, cool shells, and huge waves.

What about you? Will you live to impact the planet? Or will you spend your entire life hunting for God's blueprint, wondering if you'll ever find it or live it the right way? Will you live knowing your life has meaning, or live wishing you were making a difference?

Imagine you're on a beach. As you walk along the shoreline, the waves on your left are running up onto your feet, leaving bits of shells and sand as the water retreats back into the ocean. There are houses on your right, tall and sturdy, facing into the ocean breeze. Each step you take forward on the beach leaves a footprint...the exact shape and size of your foot. The imprint of your toes is left there for others to see. Before you walked in the sand, the beach had never experienced your step. You'd never left a mark that you'd been there. There was no traceable path of your journey along the coast. As you walk, the depth of your footprint represents the weight of your body.

You were created to make a difference in this world. You were designed to leave a unique footprint. Not five years from now... right now. Not after twenty years of seeking and hunting. Right now. Immediately.

You know, when we're old, a lot of us hope to look back on our lives and see a few people for whom we made a difference. Maybe we'll see the faces, remember experiences, and know that the lives of those few people were changed because of our own actions. But why in the world should we wait that long? Why wait until you're 85 years old to reflect on where you've left a mark, and whose life you've shaped? Why not live that way now, seek to make a difference right now in the lives of people that you love, or should be loving?

Let's not wait. Let's begin to make a difference now in the people we know, in the churches where we worship, in the jobs we work, in the schools we attend, and in the families God has given us. Let's begin leaving footprints right now. Today.

Take a look at your feet. Those two flat pieces of flesh are God's metaphors for our lives. The more we put our feet to the earth and walk the planet for God, the more lives are changed. We talk so much about being on a journey, but let's not just talk—let's actually journey. Discover who you are now so you can use who you are now for God's glory. Toss certainty and concrete living aside. Leave rules, steps, and guidelines behind you, and step off into the journey of knowing who you are. Waiting is not an option.

PUT YOUR FOOT DOWN

Do you struggle with seeking God's will? Take the next step by thinking through these questions on your own or talking about them with a friend.

• What do you think the words "searching for God's will" mean?

• What aspects of God's will are most difficult for you to grasp?

• Where have you struggled with God's will in your life?

• What do you think you'd have to "unlearn" in order to understand what God's will is?

chapter 2

WHAT IF YOU *REALLY* BELIEVED GOD LOVES YOU...

...would you love him back with your life?

I've grown uncomfortable with the phrase, "God loves you and has a wonderful plan for your life."

Well, maybe not *uncomfortable*.

Maybe I should say I've grown to really dislike the phrase.

No, not that either. How should I say this? Hmm...maybe like this...

I've grown to *hate* the phrase, "God loves you and has a wonderful plan for your life."

I'm not sure I can entirely explain why I hate that often-repeated saying. It might be that I feel uncomfortable reducing what it means to be a believer into a T-shirt slogan. I feel the same about anything marketing Jesus...Jesus bobble heads, T-shirts, bumper stickers, trendy Bibles, etc.

But maybe the real problem is that I just don't believe God wants us to think about him in such a trite way. I know God loves everyone... the lost and the found, the homeless and the wealthy, the sick and the healthy. But I don't think it's as easy as the phrase implies—"Okay, God loves me, so my life will be perfect." And I don't think God's plans for us are always easy to handle or in line with our idea of "wonderful." Sometimes God leads us into situations that feel impossible. Sometimes God's plans can be painful. Sometimes following God's plan can even put our lives at risk. But you just can't pack that truth into a tidy, easily marketed Christianese saying. You won't attract a lot of people to become followers of Jesus with the phrase, "God loves you, but if you follow him, holy cow, get ready for the pain."

Following Jesus has given my own life meaning, purpose, and a deep sense of joy. But it surely isn't always easy or convenient. In fact, if I were going to be honest, my walk with Christ has included quite a bit of tough, hard-to-deal-with faith-testing. And following Christ certainly hasn't shielded me from pain, emotional trauma, betrayal, or struggle. I can't say God's plan for me has always been wonderful.

So, God's love? Definitely, but it's not the always-easy, cotton-candy kind of love. And God's plan? Well, maybe, but it's not "wonderful" in the easy-to-swallow way we often think about it. So I'm going to take this opportunity to totally rewrite this popular Christianese phrase. Ready? Here goes...

God loves you.

There. Does it work? I think it does. Because, when you think about it, what more do we need? Relationships? Certainly, but shouldn't those flow out of the love of God? Purpose? Absolutely, but that too ought to result from our understanding of God's love. This book is about discovering your purpose in life—but that purpose begins and ends in God's love. Our purpose is to discover more of that love through our entire lives. We should be hungry to learn it, to internalize it, and to help others understand it. We should be hungry to live it which, I think, is the ultimate call on every believer's life.

I wonder if God's love *is* his perfect will. I wonder if the two are completely inseparable.

GOD'S LOVE IS THE IMAGINATION OF US

If you're like me, you need tangible stuff to understand the intangible. When I hear that I have been "lovingly created" by a caring God, the words sometimes feel too shallow. I can't touch or feel those words. I can't wrap my mind around the idea that God—the infinite, always existing Creator of all—would love me so much that he would carefully craft me into being, not to mention the millions and millions of other humans he's loved into existence.

So when I try to wrap my mind around being lovingly created, my mind goes back to when I was a kid, back when I would design and build massively creative inventions with Legos, Play-Doh, Lincoln Logs, Magnetix, and blocks. My friends and I would construct all kinds of stuff using small pieces of metal and tiny bolts, battery-powered motors with pulleys, and small snap-together pieces. All we needed were materials, imagination, and time; before long, we'd have built an intricate tower as tall as we were. After that, we'd surround it with plastic army men, ready for an attack. Then we'd dig a few broken airplanes and helicopters out of a toy box and, before long, we'd be waging an all-out-war against another tower or an invisible enemy. After we'd killed off the enemy, we'd turn on each other—and before long, everyone would be dead. Depending on who was playing, these tower wars could go on a long time. And, if the battle only lasted a few minutes, we'd usually just rebuild our towers and go at it again.

The creativity and imagination that allow us to design and invent is in us because God put it there. We were made in the image of God, and our creativity is a reflection of God's creativity. And how creative is God? He made the sourness of grapefruit, the snap of cold on your face on a winter day, the smell of fajitas, and the color orange. But the most important ingredients in God's creative laboratory set are human skin-and-bone, DNA, atoms, and molecules. He mixes those together and makes us, his much loved creations. God's creativity isn't a bland concoction of what he had left over from creating something else. There aren't levels to his passionate love of what he's created in us, like God admires some of us, loves others of us, *really* loves others. I believe God is amazed at what he's done in each of us, seeing the inside and outside of us at once and being wowed at what he's done.

The idea that we could ever fully grasp or completely understand God's love seems silly to me. I don't think it's possible to comprehend one square inch of God's love for us. It is too vast to understand, too accepting to comprehend, too unconditional to fathom. We try hard to live in ways that reflect God's love, but the truth is that all our attempts can never fully mirror his love. It is impossible to fully understand, and yet it exists in us and for us. The quest to experience God's love moves us outside ourselves and into the lives of others.

REALLY BELIEVING GOD LOVES US

I've heard a lot of students ask the same questions about God's plans in their lives. They're unsure about the direction of their next step. They fear making the wrong choices. They can't hear God clearly. But often I think these students are struggling less with questions about God's will and more with a feeling of uncertainty about God's love for them. They're afraid they're going to make a huge mistake and God won't love them anymore. They'll make the wrong choice, and God will be less interested in their lives—or they'll have to backtrack through all their bad decisions before God can ever use them again. They don't really believe God's love is unconditional or free.

Do you understand that God loves you more than you can ever comprehend? Are you aware that your mistakes won't make him turn his back? Do you know God's love isn't conditional or dependent on your emotion or your faithfulness? Seeking God's will without being grounded in God's love is like trying to ride a bike 100 miles with no tires—just metal rims. Without God's love, our life quest becomes an empty journey, and we end up trying to find a job, person, or experience to fill the void inside that can only be filled with the love of God.

What do we need to know about God's love for us?

God made us to love us.

God didn't create us so he could have robots blindly following his word or his plan. We aren't here because he's bored. Our purpose isn't to preach on street corners, sit around and wait for the rapture, or memorize the Bible. He created us to love us. Period.

I think that's frustrating for some of us, because we understand what it means to be "not loved" much more clearly than we know what it means to be loved. So when we hear that God made us to love us, we really don't understand it. Instead, we hear in our heads, "God will not hurt us" or "God won't forget us."

Why do we reduce God's love to a John 3:16 refrigerator magnet saying? God's love for us is as invasive as open heart surgery, as all-encompassing as a soaking rain shower, as bright as a lighthouse stuck on us, as encouraging as a note from our favorite teacher, as pursuing as a police chase, and as protective as full-body Kevlar. God's love is enduring, healing, protecting, and a lot more. His love chases us into the darkest corners of life and stays in those places with us.

Check out what Paul says here...

For I am convinced that neither death nor life, neither angels nor demons, neither the present nor the future, nor any powers, neither height nor depth, nor anything else in all creation, will be able to separate us from the love of God that is in Christ Jesus our Lord. (Romans 8:38-39)

Consider what God says to Isaiah—and to each of us: "See, I have engraved you on the palms of my hands..." (Isaiah 49:16). Now I don't know about you, but if there's something I absolutely have to remember, some phone number or appointment I want to be sure I keep in mind, I'll sometimes scribble it down on my hand. So what is it that God never wants to forget...what's so important to him that he writes it onto the hand of eternity? Your name is written on his hand. How much does the Creator of everything love you? That much.

We were made to serve the king who knit us together using blood and tissue and bone and muscle and loves us with an undying passion. Imagine the greatest portrait ever painted...you are much more treasured. Imagine the greatest building ever constructed...you are more grand. Imagine the most amazing natural wonder...you are more astounding. And in response to the love that brought us into being, our chief goal in life should be to use our uniqueness and skills and accomplishments to point back to God. Who we are has to glorify God first. Everything else comes after that.

Because of God's love, we can live with courage. Are you struggling with whether you should step out and do something you know God is asking you to do? Are you ready to commit to a major, job, or career path, but you're not sure God will go with you or protect you? Are you uncertain about what to give your life to? God's love gives us courage. We can do what we think he wants, or what we know he wants. We can pursue the passions God has placed within us, knowing we are secure in his love.

God made us to bring pleasure to him.

Imagine it like this: You're three, and your parents have taken you to one of those fast-food places because it's lunchtime, and you've already terrorized the house far too much today. They send you out to the play area while they order lunch. By the time they enter the enclosed playground (complete with multicolored slides, a plastic ball pit, and one of those nylon rope climby things) you've made friends with every other kid in the place. You and your new friends chase one another around, playing a modified game of tag/hide and seek/sliding contest. Your parents grab a nearby table but don't have the heart to call you over for lunch. Each time you catch a glimpse of them, they're looking at you like they've never seen you before. They're obviously amazed at you, their kid. By the time you're hungry enough to stop playing and head over to the table for lunch, the *"oh, look how cute you are"* love flows like the ketchup you dump all over your French fries.

When we really experience that kind of unconditional love from God, when we get a glimpse of the joy he feels in creating us, it moves us to respond back with love and joy to him. It's not so much an "ought to" as a "get to." We *get to* have a relationship with the Creator of the universe. We *get to* live in loving relationship with the God who loves us. We *get to* give that love back by living a life of worship to him. In everything that happens in our lives, no matter if we're cleaning toilets or playing pro sports, whether we are millionaires, homeless, or amazingly normal—our ultimate purpose is to return glory to the God who marvels at what he's created us to be.

God's love is what motivates us to act on his passion in us, because ultimately that passion brings glory to him. Our passions, callings, gifts, and desires, if they're motivated and fueled by God's love, turn the attention away from us and onto him. Do what he's calling you to do, but do it in love—otherwise you'll be an empty monument to yourself.

God made each of us perfectly unique.

There are two groups of people running around the globe spreading their opinions on what God thinks about humanity. One group seems intent on reminding us about how trashy and sinful we are. They are constantly heaping sin upon us, talking about what miserable failures we all are, and reminding us about how unworthy we are in the presence of God's greatness. They see humanity as God's junk. Oh yeah, God loves us, but his love endures through our rottenness. We are God's much-loved, fantastic disappointment.

I'm in the other camp. I believe God loves us so much that he made us perfectly unique. In love, God made every single one of us different from every other and, in love, each of us is perfect to him. We are the perfect representation of what he wants us to be. If your nose is big, if your hair is a freaky color, if you have chronically bad breath—God wanted you that way. He made you unique.

That uniqueness includes your personality, your looks, your smell, your tastes in clothes and food, your abilities...anything that makes you unlike anyone else. Your uniqueness is God's stamp of creativity. You're exactly what God had in mind when he made you. The writer of this Psalm reminds us...

For you created my inmost being; you knit me together in my mother's womb. I praise you because I am fearfully and wonderfully made; your works are wonderful, I know that full well. My frame was not hidden from you when I was made in the secret place. When I was woven together in the depths of the earth, your eyes saw my unformed body. (Psalm 139:13-16a)

God saw us as he was creating us. He could see what we would look like as he was making us. There are really important words there... *knit, fearfully and wonderfully, frame, woven, unformed.* Can you tell the author of that psalm was trying to describe the indescribable?

If your understanding of God is stale and unimaginative, then you may never discover how cool you are—because a stale boring God makes stale boring people. However, if you've embraced God's wonderful creativity, you'll see yourself as an interesting world just waiting to be discovered. Living in God's love encourages us to discover more about who he made us to be.

God built skills, abilities, and passions into each of us.

What kind of cool gifts and abilities did God give you? What passions did he place within you? How does he want you to use those things on the planet? We were created to be loved and to love God back—and the skills, abilities, and passions we've been given were placed in us so we could do that. God didn't just make us, plop us on the planet, and then walk away, waiting for us to uncover what he made us to do. He built us with passions that fuel our lives. He built us with skills and abilities, so he can call on us when he needs those skills. He gave us intelligence so we can think and reason out the things he tells us. But ultimately, the only way we can become the people God made us to be is with love. If we could all understand that living God's love is the primary goal—maybe even the *only* goal—then a lot of us would stop wondering and worrying about what we were supposed to do with our lives, or where we were supposed to go with our jobs, or what we were supposed to study in college. Isn't the purpose of our lives more biblical (and just plain easier) if we ask the simple question, "Where can I love the way God made me to love?"

THE FEAR OF GOD'S LOVE

Christians talk about God's love a lot, but we often fail at actually living it out. The truth is, many of us are afraid of what God's love will do in us. Many of us don't know what to do with homeless people— we may donate a few dollars or volunteer at the local shelter once in a while, but for the most part we don't really know how to help. We don't know what to do with the abused, the broken, or the out of work. We don't know how to take God's love into starving places, into lonely places, into rich places, or any other place where we feel uncomfortable. Poor Christians aren't confident enough in God's love to take the gospel to rich Christians. Rich believers often wedge a homeless shelter visit in between shopping trips. We don't trust God enough to really love someone of a different class, race, or religion. We're more comfortable condemning a gay man, a woman at an abortion clinic, or a meth addict than we are expressing God's love for that person. Far too many of us think God's love is something we read about in the Bible, and then we spend the rest of our time pointing fingers at everyone who doesn't "get it."

God's love is universal and for all, yet we've done our best to make it only for the people who attend church. The Bible says God loves the entire cosmos, not just the people who sit in churches, witness, or do good deeds. God loves gay people as much as he loves straight people, yet many churchgoers spend most of their time making up new rules that seek to limit God's love instead of spending their time telling people about God's all-inclusive unconditional love.

We work so hard limiting and restricting God's love both for others and for ourselves that we find it difficult to love God back. If we don't believe he loves everyone equally, or if we don't believe God loves us as deeply as he loves someone else, it's impossible to love him back—because we're trying to love the wrong thing. We're trying to love a false god who is selective with his love, one who loves us only conditionally.

I just came back from a mission trip where our students were joined with several other groups to serve the poor in Matamoras, Mexico. We worked hard all week—painting some days, sharing testimonies on other days, doing prayer walks, playing soccer, and blowing bubbles with children. Each night the adult leaders would get together and listen to one another's tales of what happened that day in our students. One story moved me, and helped me see how little I trusted God's love.

One afternoon, one of our groups spent time in prayer, asking God what he wanted them to do that afternoon to serve the people in the community where we were working. The area where we were working was really run down. Some of the people were dirty. Some were pretty scary too. The entire group felt led to go back to one old woman's house and wash her feet. So they went to the woman's house, and asked permission (in broken Spanish) to wash her feet. The woman agreed, and the group members took turns washing her feet, and the entire group sang and wept as the presence of God filled the place where they were serving.

We fear where God's love will lead us. What if God's love leads us to step into places of great poverty and need? What if it leads us into places where sin thrives? What if God's love leads us to be friends with abusive people? With homosexuals? With people who make us uncomfortable?

What if God's love leads us to wash people's feet for the rest of our lives?

Do we trust God's love enough to go where it leads us?

I know, I know...the Bible also talks about God's judgment. But the judgment of God is something *all* of us are subject to, and that's in his hands. The way I understand the New Testament, Jesus poured out love on those outside the church—and saved most of his judgment for those inside it. These days it feels like most Christians do the opposite. We Christians are patting one another on the back for how holy we are and investing a lot of time hating people who don't walk, talk, think, or vote like we do.

We also fear what God's love might cause us to see in ourselves. And, because of that, we live like God's love is not for us. It's for that guy over there or that girl who really needs it; it's for our pastor, or our best friend, or some other person we know who is really holy—but we are different. We feel we're not worthy, or we live like God could never really love us. We rule ourselves with self-hate, not godly love. We fill our emptiness with stuff...caffeine, overeating, television...anything to distract us from the conflict between the reality of how much God loves us and how rotten we feel about who we are. We cut ourselves off from others because we're certain no one could understand our confusion. We ignore God's creativity and act like it wasn't used when we were made. We live believing God loves us because he *has* to love us...God cares because he *has* to. But God's love isn't a divine afterthought. He didn't make us and then say to himself, "Well, now I *have* to love these folks."

We don't believe God enough to trust that he could genuinely love us. We don't believe God's love enough to trust that it could actually lead us to change the world.

What would happen if we totally changed our understanding of God's love and accepted it for what it is? What if we really trusted the love that engraves our names on his hands, the love that is inescapable and indescribable, the love that doesn't think we're junk, and doesn't choose some but not others? What if we woke up tomorrow morning and made it our only goal, wherever we lived or worked, to be willing to put ourselves on the line and live that love?

LIVING IN LOVE
God made us in love to return that love back to him through the way

we were created. So the big question isn't "What is God's plan for my life?" or "What job should I apply for?" The question is, "How can I best love God with my life?" Our prayer shouldn't be, "Lord, tell me what to do." It should be, "Lord, teach me today to live more in your love than I did yesterday, and use that to direct my life." Does living in God's love mean you'll want to go get a college degree? Maybe...maybe not. Does it mean you'll end up in a great paying job? Possibly...possibly not. Does it mean you'll spend the rest of your life in the same job, call, or city? You could be...you might not be.

God does love us, profoundly. And if there is any "wonderful plan" God has for each of us, it's that we live into a real experience of that love. That's God's plan for you and for me.

How do we do that? I'm certain I don't have a perfect set of steps you can follow to discover and experience God's love. I'm not sure steps even work, because steps imply that there's a way to wrench God's love for us from his hand. But I know as I've been hungry to connect with God's love, this is what has worked for me...

Silence...

My wife is an outstanding out-loud reader. When we first had kids, I was amazed at her ability to read long chapter books to the kids with great expression and incredible endurance. Some nights she would rip through three long chapters aloud. I could never do it. Every now and then I'd try to fill in as the reader, but usually my AD/HD gets the better of me, I get a little out of control, and I end up breaking everyone's concentration.

One night a few weeks ago, my wife was reading to the kids, and the kids were acting just like their dad: They were fidgeting, looking around the room, being a little disruptive. Jacqui kept reading, stopping now and then to ask them to settle down. But it was pretty obvious that, even though they were being physically still, they weren't really paying attention.

Halfway through the chapter, one of the kids said, "Wait, Mom... what just happened? I don't get how that makes any sense." To which my wife replied, "If you'd been paying attention, you'd know what was happening."

We spend so much time moving around, doing everything but being silent and listening, that in the end, we miss out on the story. God speaks his love to us in silence, but in the busyness of life, we often can't hear him. How can we know how much we're loved if we never take time to listen to the One who loves us? I've heard both God's truth and God's voice in many different people, but so often I've heard his voice as my own, in my head. The best way to hear from God is to make yourself silent. If you're struggling to hear God, whether it's about his love or about what he wants you to do with yourself...shut up!

If you really crave God's voice, you'll pursue it. God's voice and his presence are what we need if we want to know about his love. You've read a lot about God's love, but sometimes reading about it isn't enough. His love is found in his voice. Do you long to hear from God? If you do, you'll look everywhere for God's voice—in your grandparents, in your mom and dad, in your teachers and pastors. Most of all, you'll be a person who searches God's Word which is, I believe, one of the primary ways he speaks his love and desires for us.

Surrender...

I'd love to have a job where my main responsibility was to get groups of people together to experiment with different team-building games. One of my favorite exercises is the one where everyone stands in a circle, with one person in the center standing as stiff as possible. The person in the middle leans back while keeping her body stiff, and the other pass her around the circle. I've watched a lot of people freak out when they are in the center, tossing their hands all around trying to catch themselves, when there's a perfectly good group of people there to protect them from falling.

It is frightening to give up control of your life. What if you give your life over to God and he asks you to do something really scary or asks you to befriend someone you hate? What if he challenges your prejudices by placing you in situations with people of other races, economic backgrounds, or sexual preferences? What if you submit yourself to God and you end up sharing a cardboard box with a home-less man? What if you submit yourself to God and everyone hates you, you fail at everything you attempt, and you never get married?

People usually think our control issues involve fears like these. But maybe our not wanting to submit ourselves to God has nothing to do with fear. Maybe it has to do with pride—the voice in your head that says, "I'm smart. I can figure things out for myself. No one's go-ing to tell me what to do...not even God!" This attitude puts us on the same level with God. While we proud people may be willing to listen to God's "suggestions" for our lives, we find it much more difficult to admit God has better insight into our future directions.

Surrender means letting go—and I mean that. Maybe you're wor-ried about where you'll go to college. Surrender that fear. You're wor-ried about whether you'll have food to eat next week. Surrender that. You're not sure you'll have enough time to study for the important exam that's coming up. Surrender that. Surrender the deadline, the due date, the grand overarching plan you've created for your life, and even the person who's pushing you to decide about this or that. Let go of the fear that says this thing, whatever it is, is so important that your life has to stop until you've made that huge decision or passed that big milestone.

Those things stand like linebackers between God's love and us. They keep us in the tyranny of the urgent, the place where God's love gets mixed in and lost with everything else. Surrender all that to God in prayer and say to him, "This is yours," and then seek to understand his love first before you go back to that thing.

I think that's important, especially in the journey that we're on to impact the planet. How can we impact the lives of others for God when all we're really interested in is pushing our agenda through, or responding to urgent things? We can't. Let them go.

Writing about God's love isn't easy for me. When I say I'm uncomfortable with the phrase "God loves you and has a wonderful plan for your life," it's not just the "wonderful plan" part that I struggle with. I believe God loves me, but those words don't flow out of me with great ease. To be honest, I've spent a lot of my life feeling totally unlovable and completely worthless before God. I've struggled with my own self worth for much of my life, feeling like God's love is a great fairy tale. I've envied the stories of people who have lived a life fully knowing they're loved, and I've longed, my entire life, to know that God loves all of me—including my intellect, my bad attitude, my personality—everything.

I love that God does not force his way into us, even if we ask him to. Over my life I haven't felt the rush of God's love flooding me over me. I've felt tiny waves, in moments when I've most needed them. Times when I've felt my lowest, when I've felt most alone or when I've messed up in some major way, God's love has come over me and into me and has soothed what was aching. This has happened sometimes, but not all the time. In my experience God's love is also unpredictable. But his unpredictable love has become important to me. Worth waiting for. Valuable.

The world needs God's unpredictable love. Open yourself to knowing and experiencing that love in every way you can. And then, please, take it with you everywhere you go. If you will do that with your whole self, God will be glorified, and the world will be changed.

PUT YOUR FOOT DOWN
Do you have trouble believing God really loves you? Take the next step by thinking through these questions on your own or talking about them with a friend.

• How have you struggled with God's love for you?

- What's the most effective way for you to see God's love in your life?

- In what ways did God make you unique?

- How have you worked to make God's love an exclusive club?

- Name three people you could help experience God's love better.

chapter 3

WHAT IF GOD USES EVERY RELATIONSHIP AND EXPERIENCE TO SHAPE YOU...

...would you see yourself differently?

I chewed tobacco at 4-H camp when I was a kid, and I threw up. One of my buddies had a pouch of Red Man, and the other kids were putting the brown stinky leaves in their mouths, so peer pressure demanded that I try it. Three chews in, and the world began to spin. Three more, and the world spun faster...the guys circling around me, a barn in the distance, the clouds. A few more chews, and I was on my back with a wad of gross tobacco at the back of my throat. I turned sideways. I puked. And I never, ever chewed tobacco again.

I learned, through that disgusting encounter with tobacco, that I hated the taste, couldn't handle the intensity, and was not made to chew tobacco. I needed that life experience to teach me that truth. I needed it—just like I needed the time I ate shrimp (hated it), wrote my first term paper (loved it), stood on a skateboard for the first time (fell off), and picked up a guitar for the first time (enjoyed it—and eventually learned to play pretty well).

As I look back over my life, I see how God has used every experience I've lived through to shape me into the person I am today. I know he's used the family I grew up in, my friends, my wife and kids, my church, and everything else I've lived with and through to make me who I am.

But it's only recently that I've begun asking *why* God placed me in the life he has, with the relationships and experiences I've had. Think about the people in your life—your family, your friends, the people in your church and school. Why has God brought you together with these people? You're not living the life you are living by accident. God is in this. So the question is, why are you living where you are, in this place, with these people? Every relationship we have, every life experience we've had up to this point in our lives is a tool in God's hand shaping us into the people he wants us to become. There are no accidents. Where is God in where he has placed you? How is he making you into the person he wants you to be?

ALL IN THE FAMILY

God places us in the families he does to begin his process of making us into his people. I've always thought of family as being like the frame around a painting. You are a portrait that God has painted, a masterpiece—and your family is the frame that surrounds you, bringing out your natural beauty.

Of course, not every family is one of those beautiful, antique, well-oiled wooden frames. Just in case you've always thought God works only in perfect families, I've got news for you: God is at work in every family. Your family doesn't have to be perfect, beautiful, or even "normal." If you grew up in one of those healthy families where everything was picture perfect, I envy you. I grew up in a divorced family, and I resented my broken frame for the longest time. Sometimes I feel like my family frame belonged around one of those black velvet paintings at the flea market; like the ones of Elvis or of a ferocious tiger. I don't blame my parents or myself or anyone else for the damaged frame that surrounded me then, or even now. Sometimes families just fall apart. Sometimes frames are ugly. But as I look back I can definitely see God's hand in my uncomfortable family. I don't know why God has chosen to surround some of us with beautiful golden frames while others of us received rough-hewn wood frames. God puts us in the families that he does because they're the incubators he wants to use to make us into who he needs us to be.

We inherit much of our view of the world from our families. Your family unit is the first place you learn your values, your political views, your ideas about God and the church, and dozens of other life-shaping ideas. It's where you test out what you like and don't like. It's where you discover whether you prefer being alone in your room or watching TV with others in the living room. It's where you discover whether you like mowing the yard more than doing the laundry. It's where you find out if you're a neat freak or a slob.

We may want to think we just happened into our particular families, or that God just set us there randomly. But that's not true. Each of us was masterfully placed by God's hand in the exact family where he wanted us, to be raised in a certain way and to have certain experiences that shape us into the people he's designed us to be. Think of your family and their influence on you like a masterfully designed jigsaw puzzle. God brought everything together to make you who you are. Your parents, your siblings, your other relatives, your home environment—they are all pieces of the puzzle that tells the bigger story of who you are. The more you try to understand that puzzle together, asking why each piece fits the way it does, the more you understand who you are and what you're made to do.

Ask yourself: Why? Why did God put you in *that* family? Why are your parents the way they are, and how does that affect you? What about your family structure? Are you an only child? Why? Three annoying brothers? How come? And what about your family history and experiences? How have they contributed to who you've become?

Your parents' personalities and character
You're eating lunch with a few friends, and the conversation turns to parents...what they're like, what bugs you about them. One friend talks about how her dad always walks around the house in his boxers and it grosses her out. Another mentions that his mom yells constantly about his messy room and after he yells back, things usually escalate into a scream fest. Another mentions how her parents are kissing all the time and how she hopes her husband and she are still in love for that long.

And then it's your turn. What would you say?

Do you *really* know your parents? Who are they? Is your mom someone that other women call when they need womanly advice? Is your dad the local handyman; the guy the old ladies call when the screen door is busted or the garbage disposal won't work? Or, do both of your parents hit the couch after dinner at night and stay there until bedtime?

Your parents' personalities are the fuel that runs your home. They set the emotional tone and decide if you live in a yelling house, a loving house, a laughing house, or a quiet house. They determine whether you live in a brand new house with a messy lawn, a tiny apartment, or an old fixer-upper. They decide how you celebrate holidays, where you go on vacations, and most every other aspect of your home life. And you'll likely carry a lot of that with you, in ways you won't even realize. You'll think about much of the world in the same way they do.

How do the character and personalities of your parents affect your home? How has God used that environment to make you who you are? What have you learned about who you are from your parents?

Your family structure

You're at your friend's house at dinnertime and his mom invites you to stay. Everyone is eating. Every few minutes your friend's little sister gets up, goes to the fridge and pulls out a pitcher of water, and refills everyone's glass. Each time this happens, the family continues eating, as if nothing's unusual. But the next time his sister gets up, you jump up, reach over her to the fridge handle, grab the pitcher, and begin filling glasses. Because your little sister would never fill the drink glasses. At home that's *your* job.

Every family has its own structure and behavior patterns, and they affect the kind of person we'll become. If we had to share a bedroom with a brother or sister, we'll have a totally different view of college life or marriage and how to share a room with someone. If we had a sibling we always fought with, that'll affect us also. Being the oldest child shapes who you are— so does being the youngest, or the middle child, or an only child. These are all part of the family life God chose for you.

Think back to the structure that operates in your family. How has that contributed to who you are? How has being the oldest shaped your personality? How has being the youngest made you who you are? How does being an only child affect you? How has God used the structure of your family to shape you?

Your family history

Remember that family vacation where everyone argued the entire time? What about that time your family went out to dinner, and your server had the worst attitude? The close call when your mom almost drove the car into a tree, the Friday nights when your family rented movies and ate pizza in front of the television, the Christmases your grandparents spent with you—these experiences are all part of your family history, and part of your history.

The good moments we remember shape our hopes, and we look forward to repeating them when we get older. The negative ones shape our perspective, and we do our best not to repeat them. We decide what kind of person we're going to be in the future (and what kind of person we *won't* be) based on what kind of family memories we have.

What significant things have happened in your family history? What positive things have you lived through? What negative experiences has your family had? How have these experiences shaped you?

The Fingerprint of Your Outside World

Of course, it's not just your family. The second you walk through the doors of your school, step into the movie theater, sit down for lunch with a friend, or enter the church for youth group, you're opening yourself up to more experiences God uses to make you who you are.

The world outside your home forms you in a different way from how your family does. Think of the outside world as the testing ground for everything you learned inside your home. It's the place where you ask, "Is what I learned at home true?" and "Is the stuff I learned at home really who I am?" Everything you learn in the outside world is the testing ground for all of that.

But it's also another tool God uses. The time you spend with people outside of your family in places other than your home also shape who you are. Here are a few that I think are most important in framing our identities...

Friends

God uses all our relationships—the positive, encouraging friends, the annoying kid who always criticizes you, the incredibly good-looking guy, the girl who turned you down for prom—to help refine what we've learned at home. The more we hang out with friends and talk about our lives inside our homes, the more we understand the world and ourselves. God uses our friendships to shape the relational side of us. He uses them to teach us the value of knowing others. He uses friendships to help us understand the value of being known.

Everything our friends are pours into us. Some of it we think through and reject. But other stuff we see in our friends becomes who we are. Spend some time looking at your relationships through God's eyes, and ask yourself why you have the friends you do. Why do you have these particular relationships? How has God used them to make who you are and shape your thinking?

School

Your favorite teachers influence your worldview. The teachers you really dislike shape you, too. You're shaped by the grades you get, and even the way you process, learn, and remember information. Those other students who constantly challenge the way you think and what you believe influence your life experience as well. Your school is a place God can use to teach and test you. It's often where you learn about the value of hard work, study, and honesty.

Look at your school through God's eyes. What is God doing in your life through your teachers? Through your classmates? Through what you're studying? How is God using your school environment to shape who you are?

Church

Your youth group, your pastor, your friends at church, your youth pastor, the style of worship—everything you experience at church shapes you. Imagine your life without the influence of your youth group...what would it be like? Imagine if you'd never met your pastor, never sat in a Bible study with your youth pastor, never talked about God with your church friends...how would you be a different person?

Work

The moment you step across the threshold of where you work, God is using that place to help you see more about who you are, and he's possibly using you in that place to bring hope and encouragement into it. How do you work under the authority of your employer? How quickly and effectively do you accomplish the tasks placed before you? How do you work with others? Look at where you work through God's eyes. How is he using that place to shape you?

BRINGING IT ALL TOGETHER

Suppose you sat down for dinner tomorrow night, and your mom said, "Okay, gang, pass me your plates, I've prepared something really great." She brings over a big stew pot and begins spooning the contents onto your plates. But you soon see there's nothing in the pot but flour. The entire family looks at your crazy mom spooning up piles of hot flour, She looks back, mid-scoop, wondering why everyone is acting so weird, and says loudly, "It's the same stew as usual.

We're just missing a few of the ingredients."

The combination of all these influences on your life—family, friends, school, work—are kind of like a really good stew. Each individual ingredient has its own unique flavor, but when they're all mixed together in you, they create something completely unique.

Our life experiences are ingredients God uses to make all of us. Without our families and experiences, we'd just be a pan of hot flour. We'd be missing necessary ingredients that make us who we are. We could never become what God intends.

But your family and life experiences don't just shape who you are. In addition, *your family and life experiences...*

...teach you about the world.

As huge as the world is, your family, friendships, and life experiences can make it feel, well, smaller. The more we know about the world, the less scary it becomes. You know the smell and color of the ocean because you once spent a week at the beach with your friend's family. You know about the different clothing styles in different major cities because your parents have taken you there. You understand that it's cooler outside at night in the summer because you used to go camping as a child. Those realities are in your memory because you've lived them. Because you've experienced them, you can evaluate them. What experiences have you most enjoyed? Where have you been that you didn't like? What life experiences can you trust? Which ones damaged you?

...help you understand God.

Do you trust God? Is he accessible? Does he love you? Our relationships and past experiences have a lot to do with how we understand God. They are like our window to the divine. Even though the character of God doesn't change, our understanding of God does, and that is shaped by our experiences—especially in our homes. I imagine that God puts us in the families and experiences that he does because he knows the way those things will shape our understanding of who he is.

...shape your vision for the future.

Your future direction is often shaped by the people you've met and the experiences you've had. The words people speak to you, whether positive or negative, and the things you've learned about yourself—these give you perspective on what you think you can accomplish. A teacher's encouraging words about your photography might push you to pursue that passion. A friend's teasing about your singing prevents you from trying out for school musicals. Today's experiences help determine what you will do with who you are tomorrow—and every day after that.

If you want to uncover the influence your family has had on you, spend a month living with another person. It doesn't matter who...a college roommate, a spouse, your best friend at camp or on a retreat. One month living with someone else will uncover a lot about how your family has shaped you. When Jacqui and I first were married, life was good. Our emotional honeymoon lasted longer than our real one did. But when things finally settled down and we started the daily routine of living together as a couple, there was friction. Jacqui, this beautiful woman I was so fortunate to share my life with, didn't put cups away like I did. She didn't do dishes the way I did. She didn't cook the food I was used to. Her sleeping habits were different from mine. She was *different*.

For a while I felt frustrated: Why was my wife (who'd seemed so *normal*) now so weird? But after several late night talks, I realized something: As it turns out, I'm weird too. I wasn't doing things the way she was used to. And my weirdness was causing her internal conflict, too. But I now realize that Jacqui and I didn't make ourselves weird, we were just being who we were raised to be. We were the living, breathing products of our parents, our families, and our friends.

EMBRACING YOUR LIFE EXPERIENCES

Since we're all products of our unique backgrounds and experiences, we need to embrace them. Don't be the person who's too cool for where she lives, who she lives with, and what she's living through. Don't spend your life waiting until you graduate before you really begin embracing life. And, while there's no scientifically proven way to do that, here are a few ideas.

Take advantage of every single moment.
The other day I was staking cucumber bushes in the garden with my 13 year old. It was a total "dad moment" for me. As we were driving poles in the ground and tying the fences for the plants to climb, I had a strong sense that, in about four years, she and I would not be having these same kinds of moments. She'll be older and heading off to college and, at that point, we possibly won't have these opportunities. So, I told her how I felt about being there with her, about how I want to be with her forever, how I love the young woman she's becoming, and how I don't ever want her to grow up.

And she yawned. It kind of broke my heart, but I totally understood it.

It's your responsibility, right now, to take advantage of the experiences you're having. Enjoy them. Take lots of pictures. Write down your thoughts. Experience every moment, because time is fleeting, and you may not have these same opportunities again. Pay attention to what's happening in your life today, because God is using these moments to shape your identity.

Embrace who you are.
You can spend the next 20 years wishing you had a different face or different parents or a different background, or you can accept who you are and move forward from the place God has chosen to plant you. I recently heard two young girls sing the worst a cappella number I've ever heard, butchering one of my favorite songs. Even though

their singing was terrible, the performance had credibility because they performed with enthusiasm and transparency, and with a total lack of self-consciousness.

We miss part of our lives when we worry about how we look, focus on our worst features, and think negatively about ourselves. Unless you're really working on some weakness in your life, don't focus on it. Embrace who God made you to be, and then move out onto the planet, letting the world see what God has created.

Be hungry to learn more about yourself.

I love looking at family history, because I believe it tells me a lot about who I'll become. I believe that, in many ways, we will become the kind of people our parents and grandparents were. I believe that their characters, values, temperaments, and looks rest in us. As I've searched through family pictures, asked questions, and listened to long stories about the crazy things my relatives did, I haven't just learned more about them—I've learned about myself. I've discovered I have the body type of my mom's dad, the carelessness of my dad's brother, the practical side of my dad, and the talkativeness of my mom. I'm me, but a lot of who I am has come from the people who made me.

Dig into your family history. As you do that, you'll discover a lot more about your identity than you ever dreamed. The more you know about who you are, the more determined your impact on this planet will be.

Love your parents.

Yes. I said that. Love them. I know, you don't need another person telling you to respect and obey your parents. But think about the opportunity you have to influence and encourage your parents. They were your age once, and they struggle with things just like you do. They have souls that long for God just as you do. You have the opportunity to be someone in their life that encourages them to be more godly. Encourage them with what you're reading in your devotions, and ask them what they're studying in their devotions. Talk about deep things with them, and don't let them off the hook when they give you flat answers. Love them by doing things they don't ask you to do. Love them by hugging them daily. Do your best to improve their world.

Invest in the lives of others.

I said earlier that our friends pour who they are onto us. The reverse is also true—who we are eventually pours into our friends. Imagine this: You have the opportunity to impact your friends just by being who you are. The things you do, the comments you make, your character, everything you are...you can make a difference in their lives just by being yourself. You may not be able to change the entire world, but what about taking on the lives of two friends and regularly making attempts to influence them?

The other day a friend asked me what I've been reading lately. I responded that I have a few books I want to read, but I've not started them yet. She said, "Gosh, what are you waiting for? You should start reading one!" And I thought, "Yeah, I should." That simple encouragement led me into an amazing book God is using to broaden my thinking on an issue that's important to me. My friend was God's voice, getting me off my behind and encouraging me to exercise my mind. It's a little thing, but it was an important reminder for me about the impact we can have on others by doing something simple. Be the person in your friend's lives who encourages them forward, who invests in them, and who helps them become the people God created them to be.

PUT YOUR FOOT DOWN

Do you find it difficult to see God working in your relationships and experiences? Take the next step by thinking through these questions on your own or talking about them with a friend.

- How has God used your family to shape you?

- In what ways has God used your church, school, and friends to shape who you are?

- Name three relationships that have deeply impacted you.

- Name three relationships you could impact right now with who you are.

chapter 4

WHAT IF GOD GAVE YOU A TRULY UNIQUE PERSONALITY...

...would you unleash it on the planet?

Some people think hell will be smoke and fire. Others are convinced it's more like a long trip to the mall with their mom, shopping for pants. I've never been to hell, but I have found hell's annex...it's a small elevator in a Louisiana hospital.

I should tell you right now that, like many other people, I'm very uncomfortable in hospitals. Every time I step into an emergency room, I'm transported back to the times when I broke my arm or when I had tonsillitis. Hospitals smell serious and frightening. I know what they do in hospitals, and it usually involves pain, bad food, and expensive bills. I'm not interested.

But not long ago, a friend asked me to drive him to a local military hospital for some tests. I love the guy, so no place was too scary to keep me away. After we slid into our parking spot, we had a drenching walk through sheets of rain to get to the hospital itself. Then it took forever to find the right wing of the hospital and even longer to find an elevator that would take us to the right floor. When the elevator doors opened, we stepped in and headed straight to the back of the very packed metal box. I immediately became aware of the kind of people I was riding with.

You know, everyone's personality is heightened in an elevator. It doesn't make any difference whether the elevator is in a hotel, a department store, or a creepy hospital. Whenever you enter one of those tiny motorized closets, it's as if who you are gets more pronounced. Maybe it's the tight space. Our elevator that morning was just like that—one pressure-cooking metal box. The contents of our box included...

Talky Girl...who stood just opposite me. She commented on the elevator's color, temperature, smell, size, crowdedness, speed, and lighting. Nothing escaped her notice.

Creepy Corner Guy...who headed straight to the back of the elevator the minute the doors opened, pressed himself against the wall, and stood—quietly staring at each person like he was studying us for a test.

Impatient Man...who tapped on the wall of the elevator the entire eight-floor trip, his eyes continually darting back and forth between button panel and light-up-floor-reporting panel.

Annoying Complainer...who stepped in and immediately said, "Ohhh. Okay. Well, we're a little packed today, huh..." But this girl didn't stop there. It was also too cold, too small, too slow, too...elevatorish.

The Reader...who opened a book the second the doors closed and didn't look up once the entire trip.

Bored Lady...who just isn't interested in anything on the elevator. There's no person or thing interesting enough to invest eye contact on—so she just stares blankly.

Imagine you're in that elevator right now. Which of those people would you be? How would you react? How we act on elevators—and in other situations—tells a story about our personalities.

MORE THAN A TEST

Psychologists describe our personalities as a mix of chemicals and neurological synapses that are best revealed and understood by tests and experiments. There's a whole school of psychological theory that has influenced the church, encouraging people to use personality tests to help discover their Christian callings. I have huge problems with that—I think such tests rely on scientific theory more than on the power of God. When we let a test determine what we think about ourselves, what we're able to do, and even what our limits are, we've taken our search for an understanding of our personality into a quest to be told how we should act, think, or feel.

Personality tests, charts, and diagrams don't reflect the creative heart of God. They reduce it, making the intricacies of our personality discoverable through a quiz, and relegating God's creative work down into the realm of human scientific theory. Personality is not a clinical thing at all. We can't just fit "Tab A" into "Slot B." We may be able to understand some parts of our personalities that way, but not how our personalities contribute to our living out who God made us to be.

Our God-given personalities are bigger than any test. I believe our personalities are meant to be discovered and understood within the context of our lives. And God intends that we use our personalities missionally, shaping our moment in history...not with words or writings or speeches or political positions, but with our personalities, with who we are.

While I don't think any test can determine your unique personality, here are five different questions worth thinking about as you consider how God might use you.

1. How are you energized?

What gives you wings? Where are you most comfortable? Do you love being around people or would you rather be alone? What jazzes you up? What recharges your batteries? Are you a crowded-room person or a watch-a-movie-alone person?

If you love being around people, you probably enter most rooms exploding with a "Hello, folks, the party starts now!" attitude. You wander up and down the hallways of your school looking for people you haven't met yet. You start a conversation with a stranger about what music is on his iPod. And you make those quiet, want-to-be-alone types very nervous.

If you're more of a loner, you prefer the security of your dorm room where you're safe from interruptions, and where you can create an environment you work in best. You'd much rather spend time with one friend than a large group. You might make it out of the room for a few parties, but usually among people you know well and around whom you'll be most comfortable.

2. How do you think?

We all process information differently. Some of us think linearly, and study off a list. Others of us think with our hearts, and process the information we like first. Imagine you've just been given an in-class assignment. Do you read it over and immediately begin processing the information, categorizing the concepts into steps, and then create a checklist you can dutifully cross out with each completed step? Or do you look at the assignment, read the first sentence, and then notice how the first letter of each word forms its own word. Do you read the assignment and ask "What if we changed this last part to...?" or think about how funny it might sound if you read the whole sheet backward?

In short, is your personality more factual? Or are you the kind of person who tends to ignore facts for possibilities? Do you think more with your head or more with your heart?

3. How do you make choices?

What criteria do you use to decide what you like or don't like? How do you decide whether you agree with someone's opinion? Some of us lead with our hearts—we decide what we think about things based on how we feel, what makes us laugh or cry, what makes us sing. Others of us decide what we like based on what we think—we're more influenced by the numbers, the evidence, or the facts.

Suppose you're watching television with your roommate and a commercial comes on for a group that's trying to help hungry children who have recently been affected by a hurricane. You both want to do *something*—but you're someone who makes decisions with your heart, and your roommate is a head-thinking, by-the-numbers type.

Your roommate looks at you and says, "Okay, let's think about this. How can we best help those children? Is this organization really the most effective one? What's their track record of getting money to the people who need it? Isn't there some government agency that could do it better? Wouldn't they have been better off using the money they used for that commercial to help people?" And the whole time, your roommate is oblivious to the fact that you're already on the Web site and about to confirm your donation.

When it comes to decisions, some of us lead with our hearts, others lead with our heads. What about you?

4. How do you accomplish tasks?

We all get stuff done, but we get stuff done differently. Some of us are planners: Figuring out the wisest course of action, working out our schedules, and making it happen. Planners use to-do lists, calendars, goal lists, vision sheets, and organizational charts. Others are more spur-of-the-moment and move through most of their lives by what they feel needs doing right then—and they are often motivated by the pressure created when they've procrastinated themselves into a corner. They keep their lives on tiny scraps of paper scattered across their desks...ones with phone numbers and with due dates and with addresses, none of them organized with any pattern at all.

Imagine the difference like this: You've just moved into your dorm room. You began shopping weeks ago, following the combination of your own list, the list of a junior you already know at the school and the school's suggested dorm room list. You've just set up everything in your room when your new roommate walks in with seven garbage bags full of stuff he threw together in a rush this morning. Both of you will get moved in—but obviously you imagine moving into the dorm in very different ways.

5. How do you lead?

Some of us have an innate, outward leadership style that compels others to respond. Others of us are quiet leaders, choosing to lead primarily by influencing others. Still others would rather not lead at all—we prefer to play a supportive role, making our contribution by performing tasks assigned by someone else.

Imagine leadership like this: Let's say you're in your college dorm, and a few guys down the hall begin cooking hamburgers in their toaster oven. But then they walk down the hall and notice a movie they love playing in the lounge, and they sit down and totally forget about the hamburgers. Thirty minutes goes by, and their room is on fire. Even though flames are shooting under the door, one of the dummies kicks the door open, and the fire quickly spreads down the hall. Two kinds of leaders would handle that situation differently. The first kind of leader might stand up on a chair, gather everyone around him, and begin giving out assignments—ordering a few people to grab buckets of water and wet towels, sending another guy to the basement for the fire extinguisher, and telling another to call the fire department. All the activity is orchestrated by this leader guy, who naturally takes over in the crisis.

But a second kind of leader might calmly go from room to room knocking on doors and asking people to leave the dorm and quietly asking a few guys to go upstairs and tell others. Then he'd grab the fire extinguisher and head toward the fire. Before too long, the dorm is empty and the fire is out. Both leaders get the job done, but they accomplish it very differently.

What if you were in the same situation? Would you rather take charge? Would you rather have someone lead you in saving the dorm? Would you stand on a chair directing others, would you knock on doors spreading the word, or would you be the one running to grab the extinguisher?

DIFFERENT PERSONALITIES

What if you really were perfect? What if you were the kid with the movie-star good looks and the washboard abs, the student body president who aces every test and never has to worry about losing weight? What if grades were no sweat, popularity was a given, good looks were who you are, and leadership was your middle name? We tend to think that there's some perfect standard we all should be striving for. We believe God loves the outgoing, the visible leaders, the quick-thinking people. And when we think about ourselves, we're always thinking we're the worst—that God doesn't think we're as good as we could be, as outgoing as we should be, or as perfect as he wants us to be.

That's ridiculous. Keep in mind that...

There is no better personality.

We love envying others, don't we? Sometimes when we listen to friends talk about their lives, what they're accomplishing and what they're doing, we find ourselves wishing we were doing what they were. We dream of driving the same kind of car, getting the same kind of job, traveling to the same places, taking on the same challenges. Envy leads us to think that some people are better than others. We pick heroes and seek to shape ourselves into them, believing their personalities are better.

But, look. No one personality is better than another. If we all did the same stuff, this world would be very boring. I am different from you, and every person reading this sentence right now is different from every other person. Each is still important to God, but none of us are identical.

Your personality doesn't define you.

I'm a pretty quiet guy. When I go to a party, I often just stand in the corner and people-watch. Sometimes I feel pretty uncomfortable at parties, and I guess I must look uncomfortable in those situations, too. More than once, I've been at a party and someone came up to me and said, "Ahh, here by yourself, huh? Typical introvert. Are you okay?" It bugs me to be pigeonholed like that.

Those moments remind me that discovering your personality isn't about finding a niche so you can hide there. It's about discovering your gifts and strengths so you can live who you are for God's glory. Explore your personality to help you understand yourself, but don't allow a description of how you think or act become a happy castle where you live for the rest of your life.

Your personality will change over time.
I've found that many pieces of my personality—how I think, how I act in a crowd, where I choose to sit in a room—all of that (and more)—has changed. It has changed as I've gotten older, and it changes based on how I'm feeling. When I was younger, I was not outgoing at all, but I've become more outgoing as I've gotten older. I'm neater than I used to be. I learn more slowly than when I was younger. I forget more, too. As you get older, you'll change in a lot of ways. Your personality will age with you. It will become more refined, and more a part of who you are.

Your personality does not limit you.
I've heard countless people say things like, "I'm an introvert, so I can't get up and talk in front of people, " or "I'm not really a leader—shouldn't you ask someone who has an ability to get groups together?" People sometimes use their personalities as excuses for why they can't do things or why they've never accomplished anything. But personalities are what make us unique; they're not supposed to be our scapegoats. God didn't create one particular kind of person who gets things done, an ideal person, and then everyone else. All of us, with all our differences, were placed here to live out who God made us to be. We are not limited.

CHANGING THE PLANET WITH YOUR PERSONALITY
What if you commissioned an artist to paint a picture of your life, and he returned to you a boring black-and-white picture with no creativity

or color? Not one of those artistic, well-done black-and-white draw-ings...a boring, uninspired work. You'd probably look at the drawing and say, "Man, that drawing is worthless. It doesn't represent my life at all. My life isn't *that* boring, *that* colorless."

And the truth is, it's not. God made you with color and creativity. The paint and brush God uses on you was used for no one else. And your color, your personality, is the one your church and school need. It's the unique shade your family and friends need.

And because you were painted with color, to influence the world, your quest should not stop with "Hmmm, I wonder what my person-ality is?" It should continue on to asking what God wants you to do with the personality he's given you. Ask yourself why you have the sense of humor you do. Why do you process information the way you do? Why do you lead in the way you do? Your personality isn't an ac-cident; it's in you to be used to glorify the Artist who painted you the color that he did.

What if you could use your personality to change the world? What if your personality is God's desire in you to change and influ-ence situations for his glory? What if God wants you to understand your personality better so you can be a more focused influencer for his kingdom? Consider using your personality to...

Be God's difference.

Some people think the situations they encounter in life are just ran-dom happenings, things they just stumbled across accidentally. They couldn't be more wrong. Every situation we find ourselves in at home or at school is something God wants us in. I've seen this in my own life—where God has led me to someone, and I've been convinced I was the person God needed me to be for that person. God has placed you in a particular place, at a particular time, because there's some-thing about you that will make a difference in that moment. If that's true (and I really think it is) then our personality is God's gift to that moment, to shape the moment for his glory. The teacher who's feeling stressed might be the person who needs the part of your personality that is nurturing. The moment you discover your best friend just lost her grandfather is the moment God wants to use your compassion and committed friendship. The tense moment between your parents, the struggle of your pregnant friend, the hurt your sister is feeling—it doesn't matter what the situation is, your personality is God's tool. Let him use it.

Rethink.

Everything is supposed to be questioned. *Everything.* I've got days when I doubt and question and scrutinize everything. I'm sure you've got them too. I hear the guitar in my favorite song, and think I could play it better. I listen to a speaker and think I could say it better. I've got one of those personalities that criticizes much of what I see. I guess I can be pretty annoying to be around sometimes, but I think that questioning spirit can be a good thing. Too much of our world is closed to critique and opinion. Unfortunately most systems, programs, businesses, policies, and plans are set up by a handful of people who rarely ask for outside input. Too few organizations really value and use different ideas as they create and develop. Sadly, I find the church to be the institution that often seems most closed to thinking in new ways.

Our world needs rethinkers, people who will dare to use the personalities God has given them. Our world needs people who will boldly enter the world, and use who they are to change it and make it better. Be one of those people.

Challenge others.

Most people spend most of their lives without ever really opening themselves up to being challenged. They're happiest that way because it means absolutely no disruption in what they're most comfortable with—their neatly set up, overly systematized lives. But sometimes another person steps into their lives and helps them see everything just a bit differently—and it's like adding red food coloring to plain water. Sparks go off. Maybe they get defensive about the possibility of really thinking through how they live, or maybe they open up to your thinking and they change. Either way, they're challenged. But without you there, offering your idea, they would have never been led into a new way of considering their life. When we unleash our personalities into the lives of others, we become God's well-placed tool, challenging those he leads us to, bringing about change for his glory.

Leonardo da Vinci began painting his most famous work, *The Mona Lisa*, in 1502. He worked on it for four years consistently, but it still wasn't complete. When da Vinci moved from Italy to France in 1516, the painting still wasn't done. But art scholars say he worked on it for three more years there, and completed it just before his death in 1519. Do the math...that's 17 years one guy worked on his work of art. I imagine da Vinci probably got frustrated and stopped several times during those years. He allowed others to see the incomplete painting and took it on his travels (like when he took the unfinished painting with him on a visit to the French king in 1516). In all those years, he must have been influenced by countless things he noticed around him. As he took breaks from his work, new ideas for colors must have crossed his mind. Any work-in-progress is open to new influences on the author and the creation.

In the same way, God takes the unique personality he gave to each of us and shapes it through our families, friendships, and other life experiences. It takes time to make us who we are, and the changing world of our family and friends is the primary context in which God begins to paint the picture of us. It's in these relationships that we discover our personalities, who we really are.

But the art doesn't stop there. God didn't create the art-that-is-us to leave us in a closet. God wants us to take our unique personalities and life experiences—all that we are—and use them to change the world. So the question we need to ask ourselves isn't just, "Golly, how did God make me?" The question is, "How can God best use what he's made?"

And here's the cool thing about that question. We don't get to choose how God made us. But we *do* get to choose how we're used. We get to submit ourselves to the wind of his Spirit. We get to experience the places he leads us to. We get to share in the impact on his kingdom. So search out how God made you and what he made you to be, but don't stop there. Seek out opportunities to use what he's created, so his work can be displayed for everyone to see.

PUT YOUR FOOT DOWN

Can you see how God might use your unique personality to make a difference in this world? Take the next step by thinking through these questions on your own or talking about them with a friend.

- How has God used your family and friends to shape your personality?

- How would you describe your personality? Are you an outgoing thinker? An introverted partier?

- Imagine your life without your unique personality. How would your family, school, or church be different without you in it?

- Why do you think God gave you the personality he's given you?

- Name three people or places in your life you could influence with your personality.

chapter 5

WHAT IF YOU WERE REALLY GOOD AT SOMETHING...

...would you use it for God's glory?

When I was a kid, if you were cool, you had a T-shirt with some kind of iron-on decal on it. There were these T-shirt shops where the walls were covered with different iron-on pictures of dragons and animals and graphics with funny sayings. On one end of the shop they had a long counter with this huge, flat heating iron they'd use to put the decal on your shirt.

But if you were really, *really* part of the in-crowd, you didn't choose one of the decals on the wall. You bought a blank colored T-shirt and then thought up your own funny or decidedly personal saying and had the counter-iron-on person arrange that saying on the shirt using very cool colored letters. You'd stand there and wait for the letters to be arranged and then ironed onto your new shirt. And when that was done, and when they held up your new shirt with your slogan on it, you knew you were an individual...an important one, too—important enough to have a shirt with your own motto permanently attached.

I had a few shirts with animals and other decals on them. But I also had one of the really cool shirts—one that said, "Ace" on the back. I don't remember why I liked that nickname enough to put it on a shirt. But I remember thinking how cool it was that my shirt and my soul matched. I was wearing something that had meaning for me personally, and to me, that was important.

The slogans people put on their T-shirts usually represent their most optimistic selves. You don't see a lot of T-shirts that read, "I'm an alcoholic" or "Divorced three times" or "Tells too many pointless jokes." There are smart, funny, and even very disgusting T-shirt slogans, but there aren't too many that tell the real truth about how we feel about ourselves or about others.

If I had the guts to be totally honest, I might wear a shirt that says something like "Overeater" or "I have really bad breath...don't get too close." A shirt that says, "Always picked last" would be the best match for my experiences playing sports. You know what I'm talking about, I'm sure. When the teams get chosen on the playground, the athletic kids get picked first. Then the kids who can still play a little get chosen, and then the kids big enough to offer some help even though they have no skill whatsoever. Then they'd take the kid with the broken leg, then the kid in the wheelchair, and then...me. I am not exaggerating. Once, a game was delayed because two team captains got in a fight over who *had* to have me on their team. Embarrassing.

When I think about what I'm good at, I often go back to that experience of standing in line, desperately hoping the team captain would choose me. I often find I don't feel great about my ability to do much of anything. We all want to be really good at one thing, at least. We all want to be good, unmistakably good...good enough to be world famous. I've got my list...I'd like to be extremely good at playing the guitar, at lifting weights, at writing, or cooking. But if God really is The Divine Artist, why do some of us look like a Monet, and others of us look like we were painted by a dog? Would "Created by a Dog" be an appropriate T-shirt slogan for some of us, or would people laugh because *dog* is *God* spelled backward? Does God give everyone abilities that we can use to totally change the planet? Are some of us only given "lesser" abilities—like the ability to mow lawns well or be a successful greeter at Wal-Mart?

You know, there aren't a lot of Sunday school lessons taught about people in the Bible who had average abilities. There are stories about King David, Solomon, Paul, Timothy, Peter, and others whom God apparently gave amazing abilities—people who had an incredible presence and powerful influence just by being who they were. There are tons of lessons, sermons, studies, and books written about the folks who built incredible movements for God, changed the hearts of nations, and overcame tremendous obstacles to do something important for God. There aren't any stories about the guy in the back of the room skilled at knitting winter caps. That makes us average people feel a little uncomfortable talking about God using our abilities.

God gives us our abilities, combining them with passions, desires, dreams, and personality quirks that temper and refine them—all to shape us into the people he wants us to be. To be honest, I don't understand why we aren't all famous for the abilities he's given us. I don't understand why God would give two people the ability to play the guitar, yet they'd become known for it in entirely different ways. I believe the ability is there because God wants it there, and the way he uses that ability in us is also at his disposal...some of us use it for his glory on the stage, and others use it for his glory in front of our grandmothers. But either way, it's for his glory.

KNOWING YOUR ABILITIES

Maybe you're like me, and you struggle to really believe you're good at anything. I don't feel comfortable with my abilities—and talking about the areas of my life where I feel like a total wimp makes me even more uncomfortable. But we all have strengths. None of us is an empty blob with no skills at all. But sometimes it takes a little time and effort to discover what you're really good at.

When people talk about abilities, they often mean things a person can do well with very little effort—what might be called *natural abilities*. That guy who sits next to you in physics, who aces all the exams without even studying—he has a natural ability with physics. That girl who can remember lists and numbers has an ability to use her mind. That kid who makes you sick because he's really too good at tennis has a natural ability with the sport.

I had a roommate once who was naturally good at almost everything he put his mind to. Everything. Tennis, he was a pro. Studies, he remembered everything the teacher ever said. Soccer, he taught others how they could improve. Girls, he was extremely good-looking, tall, funny, smart, physically fit. I loved him, but he was so frustrating to be around because his body, packed with tons of natural ability, made my body with almost no natural ability very obvious.

When you see a need and you're able to fill it easily, that's using some of your natural ability. When someone asks for help with a car and computer and you're able to fix the problem with ease, that's natural ability. If you're naturally good at drawing or if you're skilled with numbers, those are natural abilities placed in you by God. It's okay to admit that you're good at something.

Natural abilities are often things we do with ease and with pure excitement. If you're the leader on the soccer team, if you're the lead guitar player, if you're the lead dancer, if you're the president of the math club—you've probably got natural abilities in those areas.

But natural abilities aren't always such attention-getting skills. Some of us are fantastic at quieter things. Ever met a natural organizer? How about someone naturally skilled at encouraging others? Computer techs, gardeners, planners, and tons of other natural abilities don't always lead us to the spotlight, but that doesn't mean they're less important.

Not every talent comes with ease. Abilities also include *skills you've acquired* over the years. It often starts with a spark—there's an initial interest, something you think you want to try. You try it, and the spark feels good. So you work hard, perfect that little spark, and then—it's a skill.

Other times we develop abilities out of necessity. We acquire certain skills because we have to. When I was a kid, Mom worked until 5:00-ish. She came home exhausted, so dinners were often something very simple—like macaroni and cheese or eggs. As we kids got older—and grew sick of eggs and macaroni and cheese—we'd often step in and help with the cooking. While mom was at work, I learned how to cook all kinds of things. Eventually, I got pretty good. I don't think I was born with any innate ability to be a good cook. But over time, because I needed to learn these skills, I became a good cook.

Evaluating your abilities is totally a subjective experience. It involves looking inside yourself and considering what you think you're good at, looking outside yourself at what you've proven to be good at, and talking with people who love you and will tell you the truth about your abilities. So start that process by looking at what you've done today. Consider everything you did each hour of the day. You might want to make a list with the time on the left and the activity you did or the class you attended during that hour. When you're finished, look over that list. Do you notice any natural abilities?

Next, think about your entire week. Think of those things that created a spark in you, things that might grow into something more. What did you try, see, or experience that you think might be a spark that you could develop? What were you able to accomplish successfully? What abilities have you shown off in the past week?

Then talk to people who know you. Ask your parents, youthworkers, friends, pastor, neighbors, teachers...everyone who knows you well to tell you what they think your abilities are. Write down what they say. Keep a list, and go back to it again and again, thinking through what you've heard.

Time usually tells the truth about our abilities—and that's true whether we're talking about natural talents, skills we've perfected with practice, or abilities we've acquired from necessity. So now take some time to think back even further. Think about what kinds of things you've been consistently good at, what people have complimented you about. Those are the abilities God has given you—and he wants you to find ways to continue to use them for him.

WHAT IF YOU'RE NOT GOOD AT ANYTHING?

Thinking about our abilities makes some of us want to hide. And yeah, I'm one of those hiders. Something inside us tells us we're rotten at everything we attempt or, worse, we're *average*. We find it so much easier to see other people's skills. We get caught up in comparisons. That girl is better at skiing. That guy's a better singer. That girl is better at math. That guy makes more free throws. We're ruled by the incredible abilities we see in others, and it makes us feel like we're no good at anything. You might feel like you stink at everything, but the truth is, you don't. If you find yourself stuck feeling like you're talent-less...

Put yourself out there.

Not long ago I went backpacking with a bunch of really great 15-year-olds. But there was this one kid, James, who didn't seem to have any ability at hiking at all. He needed help with his pack, his shoes were wrong, he forgot he needed a sleeping bag. He was a bit of a train wreck. On top of that, he talked the entire trip in about how tired he was, how his pack was heavy, how he didn't want to be on the trip at all but his parents had forced him to go. James was one of the most negative kids I'd ever been around. He never thought he was good at anything. When it came to any youth group games, he always opted out and sat uncomfortably in the corner. When we sat in Bible study, he never talked—you could tell from his body language that he couldn't even stand his own thoughts. He never felt good about himself or his abilities.

James complained every ten minutes throughout the entire trip. I have a fairly long fuse, but after a while, I'd had my fill and encouraged him to take up the rear of the line, the very last position, to make sure no one was left stranded in the woods. He did that—I know because I could hear him complaining the entire time he was at the back of the line.

That night we all sat around a campfire talking—about life and about the day's hike and about our expectations for the next day's hike, eating our steak-and-potato campfire food. We went to sleep very late, and I was feeling a little nervous about the next day. It was already sprinkling a little, and I could hear thunder rumbling in the distance.

I woke up early the next morning in the middle of a torrential downpour. The skies had opened, and the storm brought a wind that made our tents dance sideways. Since everyone was awake and getting soaked, I decided to cut the trip short. We made quick plans to head back to our cars where it was safe.

Of course, James was right there, complaining. He was wet. He was cold. His tent was broken. He was using the difficult situation to be more negative. What do you do with someone who just doesn't feel good about himself at all? I decided to shut him up by giving him assignments: "Forget your broken tent and help that girl with her tent. Make sure there's mud on the fire. Check the area for trash that's blown into the woods. When you're done, come back, and I'll give you more work to do."

I swear, he was done with those tasks in no time. By the time he came back to me, he'd done everything I'd asked, and he'd also put away his own tent. Best of all, he wasn't complaining. He was asking for more work.

We headed out, forming one line with adults scattered down the line making sure everyone was accounted for. James took his place at the end of the line, keeping watch and encouraging everyone. When we encountered streams that were raging like rivers, James helped organize people into human chains so we could cross them. When we encountered too-muddy-to-cross ridges, he walked ahead with one adult, seeking out a safer path.

Through adversity that kid was transformed from someone who just could not stand himself, who thought he stunk at everything, into someone who understood his abilities, someone who knew he was not junk. He discovered that his talents could make a valuable contribution to the whole group, and that made a big difference in how he thought of himself.

Sometimes difficult situations can push us to discover gifts we have that we'd never realized. Sometimes God uses those rotten moments to scream through eternity and wake us up to the fact that we really are not junk. You can be sure that God loves you even in those times when you may not be feeling very valuable. But it doesn't end there—God wants to use you, every bit as much as he wants to use the pro athlete or software developer whose skills might be much more obvious.

If you are that grumpy, useless-feeling person, try putting yourself out there for a challenge, and see what you discover about yourself.

Don't give in to negativity.

When we're feeling down, when we've failed at something we've tried, it's easy for some of us to let negative emotions take over. It's like there's something inside us that's saying: "You're no good, you're worthless, you're God's mistake." That's a lie, and it can pull us further away from what God has for us, and lead us deep into a pit where other things take over. We end up trying to hide from everyone, or we just hide our pain—until it all comes out, nasty and ugly. Fueled by these lies, some people get caught in reckless cycles of self-abuse in which they overeat, use drugs or alcohol, or indulge in other destructive behaviors—not because they really like doing those things, but because they don't like who they are. The chemical or food or whatever they're using helps them feel better for a while, until the next time they have to face themselves or their problems. Whenever they feel like they've failed—maybe they lost the game for the team, or they didn't make it into the art show—they find new ways to hate themselves, and that leads to awful downward spirals of self-abuse.

Ironically, some Christians even convince themselves that these destructive feelings of self-hate are what God intends for us. Christians are taught to deny themselves, to think less of themselves and more about Christ and others. But in some cases that truth gets horribly distorted and it makes it very easy to hide our struggles with inner pain.

If emotion is leading you into the pit, you need to find help, fast. Put this book down, pick up the phone, and call someone you can talk to. Tell them what you're feeling and let them pour themselves into you and pray for you.

CHANGING THE PLANET WITH YOUR ABILITY

I once knew a kid who was a really great skateboarder. The kid could just flat rip up the half-pipe. Every time I saw him, he had his skateboard with him. He spent every spare hour over at the skate park. But when I saw him again a few years later, he'd lost interest and had given up skating. He was serious, and he was good, but after a while, he realized that he wasn't as serious about pursuing skateboarding as he appeared. Building our passion on top of our abilities means finding the things we're good at and pursuing them no matter what. You need to spend your life perfecting those abilities. This takes time and evaluation and hard work.

Our abilities come with a high price. We've been given these weighty things, and it is our responsibility to use them to reshape the world, to revolutionize the planet. How do we do that?

Find truth-tellers.

We all live in some kind of fantasy world about our abilities. Ever heard someone singing in the shower who *couldn't* sing? Met a teacher who *couldn't* teach? All of us need people who will be honest with us, who will speak truth to us about our abilities. Call it "cruel truth," but sometimes we need other people to help really know what we're good at—and what we're *not* good at. Find people who will be honest, constructive, loving, and respectful. Most of all, find honest people who will help you understand the full extent of your ability (or inability) and who will walk with you as you develop what you're good at.

Find a teacher.

People who have been already been where we're heading can help us hone our abilities. Find someone you admire who has skills in the same area you do. Ask that person to invest in your ability, to teach you, to help you get better at what you're already good at. Find out what steps that person took to become better. Invite him or her to challenge you, to critique you, and to work with you until you're using your ability to its fullest.

Invest yourself.

Jesus tells a story in Matthew 25 about what it means to be faithful with the abilities God has given us. It's a story about three servants who were each given a certain number of coins or "talents" to invest. Jesus sums the story up by recounting the talents the servants were given and what each one did with them. And while the biblical word *talent* literally referred to the money each servant was given, the idea applies more broadly. There's something we've been given...a gift, an ability, a skill...but the responsibility of having that gift is that we are to use it, to invest it, so that when Christ returns we can say, "Look, see what we did with all you gave us." So you've got to ask yourself: Where are the places in my world where I can invest my talents to make a difference for God?

Remember humility.

If you're one of those people who seems to succeed at most everything you try, you bear a significant responsibility. No one likes the guy who walks around with his chest out, making sure everyone knows how fantastic he is. Don't be that person. Be secure in your own identity and abilities, and then use that security to influence others. Use your influence to encourage and invest in those who are still discovering their own abilities. Know what you're good at, and use that to change the planet.

Dream your ability into a new place.

If you have an ability to work on computers, don't settle for the box where you go and get a job working in the computer industry. Create a new area where you can be creative, and use your skill to develop the industry in a new direction. If your skill is sewing, don't just go sew suits, create things people can use around the home, or sew things for kids in third-world countries. Think about what you're able to do and then dream a new direction for your skill. The only thing that limits how you use your ability is you.

Take yourself out of the picture.
People who seek to use their abilities for their own fame are the celebrities of our society. They're the writers, painters, musicians, and movie stars you're talking about because they want you talking about them. They're the people who have T-shirts with their own name on them because everything about them revolves around their ability. But, you know, those people come and go. They're the here-and-gone-again people who don't really shape culture. They use the world to promote themselves.

But if you really want to shape the world with your ability, you won't make it all about you and your talents. You'll do your best to live out what Paul says here…

Offer your bodies as a living sacrifice, holy and pleasing to God. (Romans 12:1)

And here…

I have been crucified with Christ and I no longer live, but Christ lives in me. (Galatians 2:20)

In other words, you'll use your ability to serve God, not yourself. You'll surrender your talent to God, rather than seizing it for yourself to achieve fame or gain the praise of others. You'll look to make God more visible and yourself invisible. Your giftedness and abilities will bear the scars of Christ, and when people marvel at what you accomplish, they won't be singing your praise, they'll be singing God's praise.

So the question really isn't, "What are you good at?" The question is, "How are you going to reveal Jesus to others through the gift you've been given?"

PUT YOUR FOOT DOWN

How will God use your abilities? Take the next step by thinking through these questions on your own or talking about them with a friend.

- Name four natural abilities you have.

- Where did these abilities come from? Were they learned? Natural?

- What or who in your life has confirmed these abilities?

- How have you used your abilities to impact the world?

- Name three areas you can influence right now with your ability.

chapter 6

WHAT IF SPIRITUAL GIFTS WEREN'T ABOUT HOLY SPIRIT JUJU MAGIC...
...would that affect how you served the body?

I've recently rediscovered cereal...the best meal of the day. That's true no matter what time you eat it. Whenever you're eating cereal, it's the best meal of the day.

When I was a kid they used to put really great toys in cereal boxes. Do they even do that anymore? As a kid I really didn't care how the cereal tasted—I wanted the prize. Usually it was at the bottom of the box, and you had to wait until you'd eaten half the cereal before you'd get to it. (Unless your mom wasn't looking. Then you'd shove your hand to the bottom of the box and crush every piece of cereal until you found the toy.)

The problem was, you didn't really know what prize you were going to find when you reached into that box. Sometimes it was a great, mind-blowing little toy, like a ring that was also a magnifying glass or a rub-on-tattoo. If it was something you didn't have, or something you'd always wanted, that was the coolest. But other times, it was a real piece of junk. Or, worse, there was just a tiny piece of paper that promised a really great toy if you mailed in that slip of paper, four bucks, and a self-addressed-stamped-envelope.

It was always a gamble when you reached inside that cereal box. Sometimes you got a great gift; sometimes all you got was a hand covered with cereal crumbs.

Over the years I've often thought about spiritual gifts in the same way as I thought about cereal box toys. My life was like a huge cereal box into which God had placed some great treasure, a spiritual gift, and it was up to me to keep digging until I found it. Are you like me?

Have you spent time digging around the box looking for the spiritual-gift toy at the bottom? Are we all hoping to find some plastic-wrapped magic wand that will bring us spiritual success?

I'm uncomfortable writing about the Holy Spirit and the topic of spiritual gifts, mostly because there's a lot of controversy about what God's Spirit does in us. Some Christians have a very sincere belief that God's Spirit is pure power, and when that Spirit enters us, or descends on us, there are particular physical manifestations, like speaking in tongues—and if we don't have these gifts, then we "don't have the Spirit." Some contend that each believer is given only one spiritual gift; others believe we get many. Some believe the Holy Spirit is given only to select people. Some believe you have to speak in other languages; others don't.

I also have some of my own unanswered questions about spiritual gifts. When are we given these gifts? At birth? Does God ever take them away? Why would he do that? Is it a sin to not use your spiritual gift? Is it possible to use them too much? Is a spiritual gift the same thing as an ability? Is it just a spiritualized way of describing our personality?

Honestly, I've been to seminary, I've studied the Bible (some of it in the original languages), and all that, but the controversy and different understandings baffle me. It seems like God's Spirit ought to be something the church could find agreement on. It's sad that many Christians choose to let these different understandings divide us. I don't think God wants us to treat his Spirit like it's some sort of supernatural electric company, or that we're supposed to spend a lot of time trying to figure out exactly how the Spirit works. God's Spirit is mystery, and the moment we think we have it all figured out is the moment the whole thing becomes common and ordinary.

WHAT DOES SCRIPTURE SAY?

The Bible has a lot to say about the Holy Spirit. It also has a lot to say about spiritual gifts, but maybe not as much as we'd like. Despite all the discussion about God's Spirit and spiritual gifts, the Bible isn't all that descriptive.

Here's a little background. Think back...waaayyyy back...to the early church, just after Jesus left planet Earth in physical form. The apostles were telling everyone they met about Christ, and those who heard the truth were choosing to follow him. The result is that different pockets of believers were forming here and there all around Jerusalem and the rest of the Middle East. These early believers had all kinds of questions about how they were supposed to act in worship, how the church operated, how they were supposed to work together, and what different roles believers were to have within the church.

God used Paul's knowledge and wisdom to describe and define the identity of these earliest Christians. Paul wrote letters to many different groups of believers addressing a wide range of topics—and 21 of these letters are included in the New Testament. There are three primary places in these letters where Paul writes about spiritual gifts: Romans 12:6-8, 1 Corinthians 12:7-11, and Ephesians 4:11-13. But before we look at those verses, it's important to realize that Paul wasn't intending them to be a one-size-fits-all description of spiritual gifts. He wasn't trying to create an exhaustive list of every possible spiritual gift or explain how it all works. In fact, he seems to mention the particular gifts in passing. He's on one topic, he's on his way to another topic, and he talks about spiritual gifts as a way to explain what he means.

Take just a moment to look at the tone of Paul's writing in the words immediately before each passage that mentions spiritual gifts. Check out his words here...

> For by the grace given me I say to every one of you: Do not think of yourself more highly than you ought, but rather think of yourself with sober judgment, in accordance with the measure of faith God has distributed to each of you. (Romans 12:3)

And here...

But God has put the body together, giving greater honor to the parts that lacked it, so that there should be no division in the body, but that its parts should have equal concern for each other. If one part suffers, every part suffers with it; if one part is honored, every part rejoices with it. (1 Corinthians 12:24-26)

And here...

Be completely humble and gentle; be patient, bearing with one another in love. Make every effort to keep the unity of the Spirit through the bond of peace. There is one body and one Spirit—just as you were called to one hope when you were called; one Lord, one faith, one baptism; one God and Father of all, who is over all and through all and in all. (Ephesians 4:2-6)

Go back and read those three passages again. Read them over and over. You know, we sometimes speak as if God intended the Christian life to be some kind of ongoing Christmas party where we get stuff because God loves us and wants us to have stuff—and that stuff includes spiritual gifts. We think spiritual gifts are one of those *get* things—and if someone doesn't know what gift they've got, then they need to get to know it immediately.

But Paul's intent, when he lists the gifts, isn't about *getting* at all. See his words?

- Don't think of yourself more highly than you ought.
- Think of yourself with sober judgment.
- No division in the body and equal concern for each other.
- Share in each other's suffering and rejoicing.

- Be humble, gentle, and patient.
- Bear with each other in love.
- Make every effort to keep the unity.
- One body, one Spirit, one Lord, one faith, one baptism—one God.

Each time Paul mentions spiritual gifts, his primary focus is on the idea of unity within the body—that's the purpose of and the use for the spiritual gifts. Scripture says spiritual gifts are for the body of Christ, to ensure that all its members know how they contribute to unity. Spiritual gifts aren't intended to help you win some believer beauty pageant or move up the ladder of popularity in your church. (Remember humility?) You were given these gifts for a specific purpose—to support and build up the body of Christ.

I think the way we live out the gifts God gives us would change if we read those passages each day when we woke up, reminding ourselves that, within the body of Christ, our striving shouldn't be about getting or maybe even about seeking out more spiritual gifts. We should be focused on the stuff Paul focuses on in his words before he mentions gifts. We should be working hard at using what God gave us to build his body, not our own empires of humanly constructed self-worth.

THE LIST

Lists are funny things—especially when they are in the Bible. You see, we tend to think any list we read in Scripture is THE list. The final word on the subject. The ultimate authority. We think if something isn't on the list, then it's not important, not worth memorizing or studying.

Think about how we do that with the Ten Commandments, memorizing and quoting them as the final authority on Old Testament rules. We forget there's a lot of other stuff in the Old Testament that gets more attention—things like community rules, correct worship, even how the priests were supposed to dress.

Well, we do the same thing with the passages where Paul talks about spiritual gifts. We read them like Paul was listing every possible gift. And when we read those verses like that, we add them up to make a neat little list we can quote or evaluate ourselves by. I'm not sure that's what Paul ever intended.

But I do think it's helpful to consider the specific gifts Paul does mention. So when you look at this list that includes gifts Paul wrote about in his letters to the churches in Rome, Corinth, and Ephesus, ask yourself if you see yourself in any of these. (Note that the gifts of prophecy and teaching are mentioned in more than one verse, but I've listed each only once.)

Romans 12:6-8
- Prophecy (hearing God's truth and speaking it)
- Serving (helping others and caring for their needs)
- Teaching (instructing people to help them learn and grow)
- Encouragement (lifting up those who feel low)
- Giving (providing for people in need)
- Leadership (organizing and directing others)
- Mercy (offering compassion and forgiveness)

1 Corinthians 12:7-11
- Wisdom (sharing and applying insight and truth to real-life situations)
- Knowledge (retaining information)
- Faith (trust in God)
- Healing (restoring health to others)
- Miracles (performing extraordinary tasks through God's power)
- Discernment (reasoning through different options to find wisdom)
- Tongues (expressing God's Spirit by speaking a foreign or unknown tongue)
- Interpretation of Tongues (understanding when another speaks in tongues)

Ephesians 4:11-13
- Apostles (preaching and sharing the gospel)
- Evangelists (leading others to commit their lives to Christ)
- Pastors (caring for and shepherding the Christian community)

What's interesting about the gifts mentioned in these verses is the way you can see Paul's heart in them. By prefacing each "list" with the idea of unity, Paul seems to be trying to say, "Look, use who you are and what God has given you to build up Christ's body." And that focus is absolutely essential as you consider your own spiritual gift, and how it can be used in the church and the world.

IDENTIFYING YOUR SPIRITUAL GIFT

Paul wasn't offering these gifts as a litmus test for entry into the body of Christ. But he clearly felt these gifts represented important ways that God strengthens believers to serve the church. A number of tests have been created that are designed to help believers uncover their spiritual gifts. You might want to consider grabbing one of those as a way of exploring what your spiritual gift might be. But you can begin thinking about your own gifts right now.

Start by taking some time to read back through the list of gifts above. Do you feel yourself drawn to any of them? Is there anything there that your heart longs for, one that you feel might be who you are, or matches a desire you've always felt? Do any of these gifts accurately describe who you are right now? Are there any gifts that you feel certain you do not have?

As you read, mark the list like this:

- Write a + next to the ones you feel match who you are.
- Write a − next to the ones you feel aren't even close to who you are.
- Write a 0 next to the ones you're not sure about. They may match you, but you're not 100 percent certain.

After you've given some thought to what gifts you think you might have, seek out one or more people who've been important spiritual influences in your life. Explain the thinking you've done, and ask what spiritual gifts they see in you. Urge them to be honest about the gifts they don't see, too. And ask for their advice about how to uncover more about what your spiritual gift might be.

Don't forget one essential thing: *Commit—This process—To prayer.* I wrote that sentence in three separate parts because I want you to consider this deeply. Commit what you're doing to the Lord. Make this a pursuit of your life, not a pursuit to get that cereal box prize. This process of discovering and learning to use your spiritual gifts is a long one—it really does take your entire life. Please don't relegate this discovery to taking a test. And it's a process you have to commit to prayer, in a way that's most comfortable for you, in a way that makes the most sense to you. I pray aloud as I'm driving. I'm sure I look silly, but it's the best way I can communicate with God. The manner in which we pray doesn't matter—*what's most important is that we are talking to him.* If your process isn't grounded in prayer, it doesn't matter how solid or thorough it is. By including discussion with God in this, you'll be submitting yourself to the influence of the Creator.

CHANGING THE PLANET WITH YOUR SPIRITUAL GIFT

This past Sunday, I was totally distracted during worship. I stood there, tried to sing…sat there, tried to listen…but the whole time I was distracted. My eyes kept moving to the right of the church, to the door of the church library, which was standing open. Now for me, as someone with ADHD, that's a big distraction. If I'm going to concentrate, things need to be in order, pencils need to be in drawers, books put away—and doors that should be closed need to be closed.

I couldn't believe that someone had forgotten to close the door. But as my distracted mind continued to think about this, I remembered Luke, a guy who recently left our church. Just about every

Sunday, right before worship, Luke would walk up to the front of the church in a very quiet and unassuming way and close the library door. I realized that our church has felt the pinch of Luke's absence ever since he left.

That Sunday, I realized the power of one person's gift being used in the body of Christ. We don't have to use our gifts in a loud, obnoxious way.

So when you're thinking about using your gift, remember that it's all about serving the body of Christ. Your spiritual gift isn't the wow factor in your church. It isn't there to bring glory to you. It's not there in you for profit, for gain, to get dates, to bring attention to yourself in any way. It is there for the purpose of serving the body. How do you begin doing that?

Seek out a place to use your gift in your church.

Imagine you're given a pair of pliers and asked to remove all of the nails sticking out on a large wall. But instead of doing that, you toss the pliers aside, pick up a hammer, and begin pounding them in. Along the way, you make holes and dents, ruining the surface of the wall.

That's what we're doing when don't seek out places within the body to use our unique gifts. We've got something God has called us to do and equipped us to do. When we ignore it we're working against what God has planned for his people. The church you attend right now needs your gift. Look for places in your church where you can contribute. Talk to your pastor, your elders, your youth leader, your church secretary...everyone and anyone who might know where you might use your gift.

Use your gift like it's your last chance to use it.

Imagine you're about to eat the last piece of fruit you'll ever taste. Wouldn't you eat it more slowly and savor it? Sometimes we forget how amazing it is that God allows us to serve the body of Christ. But what if we really savored the opportunity to actually serve the body of Christ? What if each time we stepped into the church we treated it like it was the last time we'd ever be there, like we were about to leave one final mark there for God's kingdom? Wouldn't that change the way you serve? Wouldn't you work more carefully, serve more honestly, and seek change more enthusiastically?

Live with an attitude of selfless surrender.

We people in church love the power of the "I," and we use it all the time. "I'm leading a missions trip to the Ukraine." "I'm giving money to the homeless." "I'm leading worship today." We talk as if we think it's all about us.

My wife's grandparents are possibly the most godly people I know. They have this phrase they say all the time, and whenever I hear it, it totally throws me off kilter. We'll be talking about holiday plans or when they're visiting next, and they will *always* say, "If the Lord tarries..." So they might say, "If the Lord tarries, I'll be there this Christmas" or "If the Lord tarries, we'll be visiting with you next summer." I love that, because it's a very simple (and old-school) reminder of who's in charge.

We think we've got this life thing all figured out and we're in charge, but we're not—and the best attitude to have is one of surrender. We should be saying, "If the Lord allows," we'll be doing this or that...the trip, giving the money, using my gift in the body. That simple verbal act of surrender helps me remember that I am not in charge here, and I'm selfish to think that I am.

Use your gift in the larger body of Christ.

It's not just your local congregation that needs you. I can tell you with absolute certainty that there is a missions organization looking for someone with your gifts. There is a homeless shelter looking for someone who can do what God has enabled you to do. There are scores of ministries right now where people are praying they'll find someone with your gift. If you don't see ways to use your gift in your local congregation, consider using it elsewhere.

The church is bigger than your congregation. Ask yourself, "How can I use the gift God has given me to serve the entire church?" Seek out other Christian organizations—local, national, and international—where you can make a difference.

Risk your gift outside the body of Christ.

I know spiritual gifts are intended primarily for use in building the body of Christ, but many gifts that enrich the church can also be used to affect other's lives outside the body. Evangelism and discernment are two good examples of gifts that can be used not only within the church but also outside it. Take your gift outside the body and seek change.

Just one more thing: In the Bible, where Paul discusses "spiritual gifts," the Greek word he uses is quite different from what we tend to think of when we hear the word *gifts*. Paul uses the Greek word *charismata*, which is closely tied to the Greek word that means *grace*. That's interesting, and I think Paul's original readers would have caught the depth of which he was speaking. Just as salvation is a free gift from God, so are the spiritual gifts. These aren't things we have to earn; they are free to all—and that means they shouldn't be exploited, withheld, used for harm, or even hidden. God's grace is that aspect of his character that prevents him from destroying us, it was the motivator for him to send his son, and it's the part of God that makes him accessible to us. We have access to him because of his grace. And, with that same character and motivation, God unleashed spiritual gifts in us so that, in his grace, his body could move and work more like he wants it to work. We are saved because of his grace, and we work together under his grace, because of his grace.

Grace and gifts coming from the same word; isn't that just beautiful?

PUT YOUR FOOT DOWN

Do you struggle with seeking God's will? Take the next step by thinking through these questions on your own or talking them over with a friend.

- What gifts do you feel God has given you?

- What/who has confirmed these gifts existing in you?

- How have you used your gift to unify the body of Christ?

- Name three areas in your church where you'd like to use your gift.

chapter 7

WHAT IF YOU WERE REALLY ALLOWED TO DREAM...

...would you dance and sing and create?

When my middle daughter was much younger, she was convinced she was a ballerina.

Notice that I didn't say she thought she "was going to be a ballerina" or "with some practice and age, she'd eventually join a ballet group where she'd study under some well-known ballet teacher." None of that.

Jess was convinced she *was* a ballerina.

I'll be honest, I'm no judge of ballet skills. I can't tell the difference between a lay-up and an *entrechat*. In my mind *elevation* is a U2 song, not a soaring jump. So my ability to identify and enhance my kids' ballet abilities isn't that great. Still, I can tell when people are so passionate about something that their dreams are reality—right now. And in her mind, Jess was a ballerina.

Jess would enter our living room in her small tutu. Legs painted with pink tights. Feathery headband perched perfectly on her head. Balancing on her toes. Bouncing perfectly to the music that playing from her room...

...arms up...arms down...feet moving fast, then slow; to the right....then to the left...

...hands rippling to the left like water; arms moving to the right like a storm...

The entire family would sit and watch each step expectantly. Her graceful movements would enthrall us. We know she's not a mature, expert ballerina. We know she's got a lot to learn about ballerina-ing. But she is *our* ballerina. We are proud of her dancing, her ability, and most of all...her dreaming.

I love watching my daughter dream. If there comes a time when she's dreaming she's something else... a veterinarian, a chef, a doctor...I'll be there watching her act out that dream, too.

Jessica, my tiny ballerina, is my living lesson on the power of dreaming, and I envy her ability to dream. Dreaming is almost holy, in a way. There's something very special in our ability to ignore the typical and the negative and dream ourselves into the place God made us to live in. I'm convinced dreaming is holy. Maybe not *Holy* (with a capital "H") in the same way God is holy. But dreaming is special. It's holy in that way.

Dreaming is the flexing of our mind. It's what happens when we let "what if?" begin to guide us. Like, "What if I developed a new way to breathe in space?" and "What if I could create a car that floated?" and "What if I redesigned the microprocessor?" That might sound ridiculous to "rational" ears, but it doesn't sound silly to dreaming ears. Dreaming—that too often diminished, ignored, and forgotten part of us—is essential to living out the life God has in store for us. It is what God uses to move us forward.

Remember the passage where the disciples try to stop people from bringing the little children to Jesus? I think it's a place where Jesus is reminding us of the essentials of faith. If you read the book of Mark, right before the children are brought to Jesus, he's talking about divorce; right afterward, he confronts a rich man about his money. Smack in the middle, there's this moment...

People were bringing little children to Jesus for him to place his hands on them, but the disciples rebuked them. When Jesus saw this, he was indignant. He said to them, "Let the little children come to me, and do not hinder them, for the kingdom of God belongs to such as these." (Mark 10:13-14)

Hundreds of different scholars have taken a shot at the meaning of this passage. Can I tell you how I read it? I believe Jesus chooses the children to make a point about *possibility*. Children aren't restricted by the concept of reality. Their minds grasp the idea that things can exist that they can't see. Their minds haven't been dulled by "the facts." Everything in their minds mixes together...what they see, how they feel, what they can imagine. And I think Jesus wants the crowd to open their minds in that same way. He's telling them that what they've understood as reality for so long isn't at all what's true. At the same time he's giving them the perfect example of the essence of a true believer—a child. Children understand that possibilities are created by God. They grasp that there are possibilities that haven't been imagined yet, realities that exist beyond what we can see right now. What kind of faith does it take to see God do the impossible stuff we dream about? Childlike faith.

Dreaming is childlike instinct.
Children can't help dreaming. It happens naturally. They don't sit down and plan time to dream, or organize their thoughts appropriately so they'll dream more efficiently. Their dreams go off more like a shotgun blast or an incredible fireworks display. Kids haven't learned the grown-up rules that say dreaming isn't allowed or that it's a waste of time. Kids haven't been taught the "dreaming is impractical" lie. If you've ever watched kids on the playground, you've seen this. All they need is imagination and time...dreaming does the rest. God made you to dream—and when you allow ourselves to really dream, you'll realize dreaming is part of who you are.

Are you held back by a grown-up belief that dreams are silly? Drop that.

Dreaming is active.
Couch potatoes don't dream—unless they fall asleep in front of the TV. Real dreaming demands an active response. It does not wait for

when you have time. Kids who want to make a spaceship out of a big cardboard box don't sit quietly, waiting for a moment when they can speak intelligently with their parents about acquiring an appropriately sized cardboard box. They dig around the garage looking for boxes, under their beds searching for that huge box of markers, begging their parents to go to some store somewhere so they can buy a big box, and asking if their friends can come over to help create the world's greatest kid-made spaceship. Kids dream actively, and they bring everyone around them into the dream—because the dream is the most important thing in their lives at that moment.

Are you sitting around, passively, waiting for something magic to happen before you take your first dreaming step? Get moving!

Dreaming ignores the rules.

My six-year-old son said to me the other day, "Dad, what if a guy had six arms...", and then he went on to talk about all the things a six-armed man could do. I love that. Children don't care if they get it right or if it all makes perfect sense—they just go for it!

The older we get, the more we grow out of a world that feels flexible into a world that feels changeless and inflexible. We move from the law of anything's possible to the laws of physics. Children don't have any trouble imagining themselves riding dinosaurs or climbing up the outside of a skyscraper. But adults get hung up in all the physical, monetary, emotional, relational, and psychological barriers that stand between us and the things we dream about. Reality makes us feel like those barriers are bigger than our ability to dream, or our ability to accomplish our dreams.

But kids don't have that problem with the rules of reality. You see this rule-breaking all the time at children's performances. Imagine a Christmas performance. The entire kid-cast is on stage to sing. But then Sara notices her Nana, and the whole room can tell—both arms are raised and she's yelling "NANA!" Caleb spots a toy truck to the left of the stage and wanders over to see it. One kid in the audience is standing in the aisle, singing along with the cast. If adults were pulling off the performance, everything would smell nice and look perfect. But kids get that the dream is more important than creating a veil of perfection.

Are you holding back your dreams, trying to obey the rules? Ditch the rules.

Dreaming stretches us.

"Someday I will visit the Eiffel Tower," isn't much of a dream if you've already been there. Dreams are surrounded by other words… *uncomfortable, huge, enthusiastic, difficult.* The problem is, our "dreams" tend to be more vanilla, more "I want to visit the White House" than "I want to be President of the United States." And that's usually our own fault. We've allowed ourselves to play it safe, to slip into dreaming-mediocrity. We don't push ourselves to think up the impossible.

My kids taught me this lesson last year, in the middle of a very hot summer. They had this grand idea that sounded both totally kid-friendly and terribly dangerous. In our backyard we have both a trampoline and a cheap above-ground pool. One day, after swimming for hours, all three of my kids came inside and started begging me to drag the trampoline over to the pool so they could…well, I'm sure you can guess the rest. At first, I went 100 percent dad on them, listing the countless things that could go wrong….the broken legs, the busted-out teeth, the ambulance trips, the calls for kidney donors, etc. They begged, and begged, and eventually I did the stupidest thing ever. I went outside and pulled the trampoline over next to the pool. Not only that, but then I went inside and put on my own bathing suit.

Turns out, we had an amazing time—all of us—seeing who could jump the highest, contort their bodies the best, and jump the farthest. I would never have dreamed of pulling the trampoline next to the pool. I'm glad I listened to my kids. They were right.

Are your dreams challenging you to become something new and different? If your dreams don't do that, delete them.

Dreaming is optimistic.
It's impossible to dream with an "it can't be done" attitude. Dreaming demands an "anything is possible" attitude. Don't worry about limits, money, appropriateness, time, or your age. It doesn't matter if your dream needs seven things invented before you can ever do it. It doesn't matter if you need to meet several high-powered people before your 18th birthday. If your dream is to use Mars as a space station, who cares if no human has been to Mars yet? Optimism motivates dreaming.

Dreamers get such a bad rap in our culture. Their heads are in the clouds. They don't live in the "real world." But that's not true. Dreamers are people who notice *possibility*. They understand *potential*. They fully realize that ideas *can* change the world.

And before you say it, let me say it for you...there are realities. We are all limited. We can't all get elected president, star in movies, write bestsellers, pitch in the World Series, build a log cabin, start a restaurant, and save the whales. But you know, even as I say that, I feel kind of conflicted. Of course there are limits, but who says what those limits are? Who sets the boundaries on possibility?

The best thing about dreaming is that as we move toward accomplishing the great thing we've set out to do, God uses that momentum and guides us to where he needs us. Sometimes, he takes us to the exact place we'd dreamed. Other times he reshapes that dream and takes us down another road. But the whole time, we're moving, and God is using that.

Are people with "you'll never" attitudes trying to limit how far your dreams can take you? Fire them.

DREAMER-HATERS
I've got to be honest with you. The world isn't always easy for dream-

ers. As a father I worry about my dancing daughter. I worry that some-day, someone will tell her that she's not that good, that she "can't," that she'll never really be a ballerina. I know there are people in this world who love to be too honest, who love telling the "truth" in a way that discourages. I hate that there are people who drop honesty like a bomb, filling their speech with "You'll nevers" and "You can'ts."

I had a high-school counselor who was convinced I was—and al-ways would be—a failure. She seemed to think I was the stupidest, least talented person who'd ever lived. I'd sign up for a difficult class, and she'd reschedule me for an easier one. I'd talk about applying to a college, and she'd suggest I enroll in the military since it is "good for people who can't handle college." When I actually applied to a college, it took several calls and visits to her office before she was finally willing to send my transcripts.

When I finally made it into college, every failed class (yeah, there were several) fulfilled what I thought were her expectations. When-ever I struggled with a class, I could hear her saying, "Tim, I told you that you weren't college material." Every failure was a confirmation of her lack of faith in me, and it proved that I really was incredibly stupid, just like she believed.

Dreams are like targets—seems like everyone wants to shoot at them. The moment we dream, someone's there to tell us our dream is stupid, worthless, inappropriate, impossible, or useless. We're shot at by teachers who don't see our dream as clearly as we do. By par-ents stuck in their own sense of practicality. By friends who love *their* dreams but aren't willing to respect ours. And by others who aban-doned their own dreams long ago, and are eager for us to join them so they feel better about the deadness they're living in.

So I want to encourage you. Keep dreaming. Don't succumb to the thinking that says dreamers are the fluff at the edges of society. Commit yourself to seeing this world with the dreaming eyes of a child.

THE DREAMING PROCESS

I go to church with technically-minded, mostly introverted, realistic dreamers. Many of the adult men in my church have PhDs in engineering, math, computer science, or some other technical discipline. These guys have spent their lives educating the next generation of students in the details of joining materials to make bridges, creating circuit boards for solar-powered radios, or building light aircraft used to deliver supplies to missionaries. If you stand around my church on a Sunday morning and listen to the conversations that these men have with students, or listen to the students talking to each other, you'll likely hear the following statements:

Have you thought about...

Another way could be...

What if you redid it this way...

Try doing it backward...

Why can't we...

Here's how we can modify that...

After church last Sunday, I listened to two guys talking about the process of changing a standard car engine into an engine that ran off water. It began with a *what if?* and ended with a *that's how you could do it*. Moments before that I stood talking with a young man who dreamed of turning his expertise in computer science into a position working with a missions organization, aiding in Bible translation. A week or two before that I was listening to a few people talk about how infinity really is an actual number. These folks don't get lots of media attention, but they are the dreamers who move the world forward with their innovative designs and ideas. Many of them deliver papers at technology conferences, helping the scientific world rethink the framework of some of its ideas. Several of them re-dream how deeply technology can be used in our lives. Many of them are outside-the-box thinkers, refusing to settle for what's already been invented, desiring to dream.

I have to tell you, I'm way out of my league around them. I'm not a techie, I'm pretty bad with numbers, and I don't do well with scientific theory. But I get their dreaming. It's infectious, and after watching and listening to these people for more than ten years, I'm convinced there's not much difference between the way a scientist dreams and the way a kid with a cardboard box dreams. Perhaps all real dreaming—dreaming that really ends up with feet—can be thought of as happening like this...

1. I Wonder...

This is the moment where our minds wander into uncharted territory, exploring the land of possibilities. *I wonder* moments are born out of wild abandon, discomfort, and a desire for something better. "I wonder if we could rig the car to run on water" is birthed after seeing how expensive gas is.

All of us have *I wonder* moments. We have them when we're talking politics, when we're overloaded with laundry, and when we're stuck in line at a gourmet coffee shop. But we've been taught to ignore them with the idea that they're just a waste of time. Here's an assignment: Tomorrow, pay attention to at least one time you begin dreaming with an "I wonder." And when you begin to think that way, don't ignore it—dream a little, think it through a bit, and consider all of the possibilities your mind brings in. If you do that one time tomorrow, you'll notice two more "I wonders" the next day and, before you know it, I bet you'll be dreaming regularly.

Oh, and by the way...I wonder how many of God's dreams in us begin with an "I wonder." I wonder if that's how God births his call in the hearts of missionaries. I wonder if that's how God gets ahold of us and begins leading us in his direction.

2. What If...

When "I wonder" takes the first step out of the idea factory and into the world of the real, it becomes a "What if." What if we really put the "I Wonder" into action? What would happen? What would change?

Would we sleep longer? Would we get more done? Would we make more money? Would more people hear the truth about Christ? "What if" looks at an established thing...the economy, your job, your walk with God, anything, and reenvisions it as a changed thing. If I changed this or that, what would the overall picture look like? Would things be different? Would things change?

"What ifs" are important. They're the air under the wings of a dream. You can dream all you want, ask a thousand "I wonders," and paint all kinds of pie in the sky pictures, but until you ask a healthy "what if," full of life and potential, nothing will happen. That's true whether you're talking about getting into college, buying a car, asking someone on a date, or changing the world. You dream the dream, but then you have to take action for the thing to become a reality. What if you really asked that person on a date? What if you applied to the college you dream of getting into? What if you went for that job you've been wanting? What if you stepped out to change the world? What would happen in your life, to others' lives, or to the entire world? Dreams need your "what if" to become a reality.

3. I Think I Will...
Combine the questioning of "I wonder" with the desire of "what if," and "I think I will" is born. This is where you've dreamed and thought yourself into a place where you have to do something. *"I Think I Will"* is the moment when dreams become a reality, or at least try to find their way into reality.

Ever wonder what it is that allows some people to accomplish their dreams? I think it's that these folks don't allow others to step all over what God has placed in their hearts. They don't stop with the idea. They're willing to risk everything to lift their dreams off the ground.

Interested in making your dream a reality? Be willing to risk everything that's important, and be willing to look a little silly. Allow yourself to wander into the area of possibility, a place inhabited by inventors, artists, engineers, developers, and great thinkers, and see what God has for you.

I learned a lesson about the power of such possibility when I was 14 years old. I wanted to get a job and make some extra money, but I wasn't interested in mowing lawns or delivering papers. So I began to dream: What if I started my own company and began working to make my own money with my own idea?

I invited local businesses to purchase advertising space on a big sandwich board that I promised to wear around town every day during lunch. Some people thought it was a silly idea. At first, just one candy shop took me up on the offer and bought ad space. But before long, my board was full, and so was my pocket. I also started getting letters. I got one from a city judge and a few from local businesses, thanking me for giving them a vision for what young people can do with their free time. There was an article about me in the local newspaper, and that spurred more letters. Later I was featured in an op-ed piece about students making a difference. My crazy dream for making a little extra money influenced my city.

That experience is part of the reason I'm crazy enough to believe that one person's dream can influence the world. My dream was selfish—I was just trying to make money. What if you set out to dream up and pursue a totally selfless dream? What would happen if you took up solving poverty and starvation as your dream? What if you dreamed a way to put more people to work, dreamed a way to cure AIDS, dreamed a way to help people out of debt more effectively, dreamed a way to stop human trafficking? What could change because of your selfless dream?

CHANGING THE PLANET WITH YOUR DREAMS

When we talk about dreaming, we often think of stories like "Jack and the Beanstalk"—where a poor kid trades his family's only cow for a few beans, believing the beans are magic. Such fables make us feel like dreaming is silly. And honestly, some Bible stories aren't really encouraging for dreamers. Joseph did exactly what God dreamed, and his life had a long, difficult stretch. Whether you're a natural dreamer, or you struggle with dreaming, there are things that you can do to develop the dreamer-side of you. You don't need magic beans. Everyone can dream. How do you change the world with your dreams?

Recognize the dreams you already have.

I've talked with a lot of people who don't realize they're already dreaming. They have big ideas, but they diminish those ideas, call them silly, and ignore them. They're discounting what's happening in them already. Pay attention to the dreams that are in your heart right now. Even though they may feel crazy, they're not. Nurture your inner dreamer by finding other dreamers and hanging out with them. Spend time with people who inspire you to think outside the box. Share your dreams with these people and allow them to push you, give you feedback, and dream with you. Look for people who talk about their big ideas, who have their heads in the clouds.

Find a dreaming space.

We Christians have places we pray, places we think and reflect, even favorite places we read and study. What about places to dream? If dreaming is important to you, you'll find places where you can do it, like a closet, your bedroom, a coffee shop, or your grandparents' house. I seem to dream best while I'm mowing my lawn. Great thoughts come to mind when I'm involved in clearing my land and cutting the grass. The most important thing is to have the attitude of a dreamer, and sometimes having a particular place where you dream can be helpful.

Make a dreaming list.

You know what we do? We forget what we dream about. Few dreams stay in our consciousness for too long. We're passionate about them, and then we let them fade away. What would happen if you wrote down every "what if" you had for an entire year? How long would your list be? What would be on the list?

I'm a fan of lists anyway. I often create lists of things I'd like to see happen in my life, things I'd like to accomplish, and things I'd love to invest myself in creating. For a long time my wife and I kept a dreaming list that we called our "please God" list. They were things we wanted to see in our lives or the lives of others. We'd spend time praying through the list and committing it to God, allowing him to sift through the things we thought were important, and lead us to the things he wanted us to do. God did some amazing things in our life through praying about that list. But the best thing about that list was that it kept our dreaming always before us. Each time we prayed, we had to look back over and think about what we'd been dreaming about.

That's the power of a dreaming list. If your dreams are important, you'll write them down and look them over and over. So make a list, put it where you can see it all the time, and pray through it.

Tell people.

Yep, that's right, I said it. Tell other people your dreams. Announce them to your friends. Don't walk around boldly proclaiming your dreams to anyone who'll listen, like a psychotic street-corner preacher. Instead, drop them into conversations. Insert a few well-placed "what ifs" into a lunchtime conversation. Toss out a few "why don't we" statements, and see what your friends say. Chances are you'll end up in conversations where others join you in dreaming aloud. Put your dreams out in the open for your friends to see and let them be inspired to dream along with you.

I have a very good friend who is an engineering professor with a real passion for helping people. It's his nature to reach out, to be concerned for others. I have not met too many other people who combine such a genuine overflowing compassion for people with an ability to actually help them. He's not one of those guys who sits back and watches others struggle. He dives in and helps.

Not too long ago, God turned one of my friend's "what ifs" back on him, offering him a chance to unite his passionate heart for others and his engineering talent. One of his students came back from a trip to an impoverished country and was talking about the incredible suffering he'd seen there, especially among people who'd lost their legs. It was a nation where walking was the primary mode of transport, and medical facilities were quite limited. That conversation sparked my friend to ask, "What if we used our talents to make artificial legs for these people?" That idea led to a meeting with several other people at the university, and then another meeting with a few willing students who formed a design team. That led to prototypes, which led to tests, which led to more prototypes. Dreamers got together with engineers and medical professionals and built working artificial legs. Talks with doctors in third-world countries began, teams were trained, and trips were planned. The team has now been to several countries, showing up with materials, tools, and a burning passion to help hurting people. They have not only built artificial legs there but also trained people in those countries to continue that work, changing the lives of dozens of people.

All of that began with a simple "what if." What if we got a few engineering smarties together to use their talents to change the lives of people who are missing legs? What if we created artificial legs that were workable, easily made, and extremely durable? What if we refined the design, took the limbs and process to the people of that country, and taught them how to make the legs?

A dreamy "what if" has the power to change the world.

What's *your* "what if"?

PUT YOUR FOOT DOWN

What about your dreams? Take the next step by thinking through these questions on your own or talking them over with a friend.

• What is the biggest obstacle when you try to dream?

• Who are some of the dreamkillers you've faced?

• What people do you know who love to dream, and who live out those dreams? What can you learn from those people?

• Name three dreams you have right now.

• What places, situations, and people can you affect with your dreams right now?

chapter 8

WHAT IF YOU REALLY LIVED YOUR PASSION...

...would you use it to change the world?

I used to *love* racing BMX bikes.

Now I know that the moment I mention BMX racing, slap an "I used to..." on the beginning of the sentence, and then follow up with any story about a race, my broken bones, what I could do on the track, or anything else, it looks like I'm trying too hard to seem cool and relate to people younger than I am.

But the truth is—hard as it might be to believe given my lack of coordination and the spare tire I now have around my middle—I used to love bike racing. I loved the adrenaline coursing through my body as I waited for the lights to signal the drop of the gate. The best moment for me was always the first ten turns of the pedals, as all the guys raced toward the first jump, on into the first hairpin turn. A lot of races are won and lost in those first couple of seconds. But the entire race was an incredible experience of feeling completely alive, a little terrified, and fully challenged. There is nothing like competitor facing competitors, with your mom watching in the stands and that girl you like watching, too, and all the while knowing that when the race was over, you'd either have a trophy, a face full of dirt, or dented pride.

I raced against Marty Phillips a lot. He was the poorest kid on my biking team, and probably the poorest kid in my school. He'd show up to hang out at the bike shop on Saturdays when all of us bike-racing kids were there, and he hadn't eaten, or he'd have a flat and couldn't afford a tube or whatever. I think kids can tell when one of their friends doesn't have much money, even if they don't talk about it. We could tell he was poor.

So anyway, Marty and I raced a lot. Well, that's not quite true. We entered a lot of the same races. I put my bike up against the same gate as Marty. I waited for the same green-gate-dropping-light that Marty waited for, and maybe, technically, we raced together. But the minute the gate dropped, Marty was off. I don't mean he jumped out ahead and stayed one bike length in front of the rest of us. I mean, before most of us made it to the second jump, Marty was drinking water at the finish line and winking at our girlfriends.

I remember standing at the top of the starting gate mound before a race several cities away along with Marty and a bunch of guys from several other teams. We were waiting for the race to start, and doing that pre-race psych-out verbal evaluation of the track. One kid looked at Marty's bike—with its worn-down grips, a broken-off spoke keeping his brake lever in place, and a wildly unattractive assortment of very used parts—and saying, "Wow, man, kinda cheese-co" which, when I was a kid, meant "Your bike is a hunk of poo." And I remember Marty just looking at the kid, setting himself up for the start of the race, and balancing steady against the gate, focusing down the track like a million dollars were waiting for him at the end.

Ninety seconds later, Marty had blown us all away, and the cheese-co-exclaiming kid had been BMX-schooled, Marty-style.

Marty practiced all the time. It didn't matter that his bike was junk. He didn't care that he hadn't eaten since yesterday. He wasn't hung up on the fact that his parents couldn't afford cool racing clothes and couldn't drive him to the races. Marty would always find a way to practice. We'd see him around town after school bunny-hopping curbs, using handicapped ramps as jumps, riding power-wheelies. Nothing stood in the way of his desire to ride his bike and get better at it.

INVESTING IN YOUR PASSION

Marty had something we all want: The ability to fully invest himself in something he truly loved. Marty was able to silence all of the other competing voices in his head…the ones that told him he should forget about bikes so he could study harder, the ones that encouraged him to sit on the couch and channel surf, and the ones that told him he'd never be as good as the other guy. Marty lived that wonderful example that passion will come out in us if we'll let it.

But passion isn't just liking something, like you enjoy surfing, or you like to install kitchen sinks. Passion is created when the dreams God gives us take root in our lives. God is at the center of that, working out in us that desire to press forward with our passion. Exactly how God does it and when he chooses to do it are mysteries.

God gives passion because he sees who you are, what you're made to do, and how he can use you to change and shape the world. God places the passion in us, but then he leaves it to us to develop and use it. Passion is that unbridled thing that God gives us to live without control.

Passion is…

…a dream with legs.

There a difference between dreaming and passion. Dreaming is liquid, but passion is a rock-solid commitment to something you love. The two often look similar, but they're not the same thing.

Suppose you've always loved computer games. You appreciate the way computer games work…they match the way you think—multifaceted, character-driven, graphics-oriented, with a love for strategy. You've always enjoyed messing around on the computer, but you never really gave much thought to doing it full time. Then, in your free time, you download software to create your own first-person adventure game. You're immediately hooked and spend all your free time working on your new project. You finish it and pass it around to friends, who are mildly impressed.

With that little bit of ability and skill under your belt, you sign up for a Computer Graphics class at your local community college. Twenty minutes into the first session, you realize you have a stronger understanding of gaming than anyone else in the class. It doesn't stop there...you connect with other game developers in your area, you meet with gaming lovers at gaming conventions, you get to know well-connected people. Along the way you realize you really do have an exceptional mix of skill, knowledge, and creativity. That is dreaming-passion in action.

...what you are already doing.

People ask you all the time "What are you most passionate about?"—but that's not the right question, or at least it's not the entire question. The real question is, "What are you passionate about, and how are you living that passion out in your life right now?"

Suppose you feel passionate about serving the homeless people in the inner city, and you tell them exactly that. But you're not doing anything right now that connects to that concern for the homeless. If you're not involved, how could you really be passionate about that?

I meet people all the time who tell me they want to write. "I'm so passionate about writing," they'll say. "I have something to say, and I'm a good communicator." They'll ask me for advice, and I usually ask what they're writing right now. I can't tell you how many times the person on the other side of that conversation says, "Well, I'm not writing anything in particular right now. I'd just really like to write. I'm passionate about getting my thoughts down on paper."

I usually try to push them a little. "Are you blogging? Do you journal? Do you keep tiny scraps of paper where you keep these thoughts? Are there endless sheets of either organized or disorganized papers where you have been writing?" And again, very often they'll not have been writing at all. They have a grand concept of what could be, and they've translated that in their head as their passion. But writing isn't their passion because they are not doing it. Same goes for anything you "want" to do but aren't doing right now. How can you be passionate about something if you're not making the time to do it right now?

Passion isn't necessarily what makes you happy. It isn't always something that will make you rich. It is not something that you like to imagine yourself doing. Passion is where you are investing your time right now. If you have something in your life that you call your passion and you haven't done it this week, I have news for you: It's not your passion.

...*what you'd give your life to if you didn't have to earn money.*
If I asked you what you love doing more than anything else, what would you say? Listening to music? Studying art? Creating machines? Designing new flavors of bubble gum? Pondering deep space?

Growing up, my mom sewed just about all our clothes. She never attempted underwear or socks, but she tried everything else. I'd go to school wearing weird print shirts she'd made from a pattern, jeans with crazy patches on the knees, and homemade jackets. She also tried her hand at knitting sweaters, coasters, and hot-pads. My mom still sews. These days the people where she lives call her "The Doll Lady," and she spends each warm Ohio Saturday morning sitting at a card table selling dolls and puppets she's spent all week sewing. Mom doesn't make much money doing that—certainly not enough to make a living on. She sews because she loves it. I would say my mom *has* to sew—because if she didn't she might stop breathing.

And to me, that is the epitome of passion. When you desire to do something so much that it doesn't matter whether you get paid or not, that's passion. When you love doing something and it becomes that thing you do your entire life—in your off-hours, on weekends, and maybe as an occupation—that's passion.

There are no rules defining what you're allowed to love doing with your life. Reasonable people, those who have limited themselves to a predictable life, classify their lives and base their decisions on what's most profitable, what will get them the bigger house, what will buy them the nicest car or the best vacation. But surrendering yourself to what you love is different. It doesn't necessarily follow a known path or a series of answered questions. Just because it feels like uncharted territory, that doesn't mean it's the wrong direction.

...not dependent on the opinions of your parents, siblings, or friends.
The person who takes over the family business because they've been bred to do that their entire lives is not necessarily living with passion. The person who becomes a doctor because his dad always wanted him to be a doctor is not living with passion, even if he's a great doctor. The person who starts a family after college gradua-tion, because that's what her mom did after college graduation, is not living with passion.

Our families and friends can be God's miracle-fertilizer, helping us grow into the people he wants us to be. But our families don't de-termine our passion. And we don't have to get our friends' approval in order to live what we love doing. They may be the people who help you discover what your passion is, but once you discover it, it isn't dependent on them. They are not in charge of it; they do not own it; it is not theirs. Your siblings might possibly help hone your ability to deal with difficult people, but they don't make the decisions about how you ought to use your passion for mediating arguments between difficult people. Your family shouldn't be the place where your pas-sion is stunted, drowned, diminished, or controlled.

...God's tool to change the world.
I know a kid who had this desire to reach out to people in China. He wanted to go on a mission trip there, but couldn't get his Christian university to form a team to go there during their typical spring break outreach trips. So, after talking with administrator after administra-tor, and after getting fed up with all the negative responses, the guy began planning his own trip. Soon people were asking if they could join him on the trip. Before long there were more than 15 people go-ing on the trip. When it was all over, he and his team had reached

several provinces in China with the Gospel. And it all happened because he didn't give up on his passion.

Your passion isn't an accident. It's not a whim or a silly dream. It's in you for God to use. Don't give up on what God has put in you.

HOW A DREAM BECOMES A PASSION

In the last chapter we talked about the dreams God gives us and how we live out those dreams. Passion is the next step after dreaming. The two go together. First, we dream. We respond to the dream God places in us. Once the dream finds a home in our soul, a passion is born. It becomes something we have to do, something we're uncontrollably attracted to doing. A dream like "I want to climb Mt. McKinley" stands out there like a goal with a bullhorn, calling us to hike where we are, buy rockclimbing shoes, get a backpacking club together. The more we attempt to reach that dream, the more our passion builds, and the more our dreaming and passion work together until one day we are standing on top of that mountain.

Dreaming and passion belong together because they're part of the same "what if" thinking God has built into us. Call it the *Divine Power of Possibility* that God has built into each of us. And God has put these "what if" questions in us, not so we can create something that glorifies ourselves, but so that we can partner with him in advancing his kingdom, in moving his creation forward. Imagine that: God has built his creation with the ability for us to move it forward, all for the purpose of continually offering praise to him for the ability he's given us, and for what he accomplishes through us.

Knowing your passion isn't just the result of taking a test, but you can begin to identify what you truly love doing by thinking through a few questions. So, with that same, holy *What If* in mind, let me toss a few at you...

- What if there were no rules...for anything, except natural laws, the laws of physics? What if there weren't any rules about how far you could travel, how deep into the sea you could go, how deep into space you could explore, how far you felt allowed to walk, what you were able to create? What would you love doing? What would you spend your life pursuing? If you could set aside every rule you've ever heard, what could God do in and through you?

• What if you were not limited...by anything? What if your knowledge didn't limit you? What if your size didn't matter? What if you weren't held back by lack of money or ability or training or time or education? What if your grades weren't a factor, and didn't keep you from stepping out and testing your passion? How would you invest your time? You know, God has given us all a limited number of days in this life. How would you like to use the time God has given to you? What would you love to accomplish?

• What if your age were not a factor? What if you could be wise despite your youth, or athletic despite your age? What if you could lead a group of people fifteen years older than you are, or wrangle a group of young leaders? What would you accomplish if your age didn't limit you?

• What if the moment in time you are living in did not hinder you? What if it wasn't a problem that the technology you feel you need to put feet to your passion wasn't developed yet? What if you had the ability to overcome obstacles and make things happen despite difficult circumstances? What if your absent parent didn't hinder you? What if your family situation encouraged you to move forward? What would you build, create, or dream into existence?

Levelheaded businesspeople who live their lives charting each day on organizers and spreadsheets may tell you that this kind of thinking—seeking to actually live your passion—is a silly attempt to live a fantasy. But look, we don't care about those stodgy people.

All they're doing is making the world more boring and predictable. The only way you'll ever move into the place of living your passion, other than a divine miracle of God, is by asking those what ifs, and then seeking to put those what ifs into action. You could be boring and stodgy, and stay stuck in that ordinary place where nothing real happens in your life. Or, you can take hold of what you already know you love, and live it to its fullest.

CHANGING THE PLANET WITH YOUR PASSION

When you live what you love doing, people are drawn to you. Our world is so attracted to musicians, actors, and athletes, but I don't think that's always because they're famous or successful. It's because we love seeing the way they love what they're doing. Have you ever been around someone who loves his job? These people are infectious, and you can't help sharing in their joy. But the same goes for being around people who hate their jobs, despise their lives, and can't stand where they are. Spend much time with those people and you'll be right there in the dumps with them.

And that's one of the most important aspects of living your passion. Sure, there are lots of ways living your passion will affect you, giving your life meaning and purpose. But the main reason to live your passion is the effect it has on others. Your passion changes other people.

The world is looking for passionate people who will connect with other passionate people committed to changing the world. We've all had enough of people living blandly with their eyes shut. How do you change the world with your passion?

Offer it to God.

What's the right first step? You've got it—leave it at God's feet. You can do that in whatever way you feel connects you most with God. As a way of expressing my desire to offer my passion to God, I sometimes will burn something that represents that part of my life. I'll go to a safe place where I won't set the entire neighborhood on fire, spend a few minutes praying and asking God to take what I have, and then I'll burn it, offering it over and over to God as it burns. I've done this with poetry, book manuscripts, and a few thoughts. It's my way of showing God I'm taking this seriously, and it creates for me a memorable moment I'll never forget. You need to do the same. Commit your passion to God. Offer it to him in prayer, as a tool to be used for his glory. Let him know you're available and willing to be used.

Step out into the world.

There are a lot of people who are afraid to show who they really are. They're fantastic guitarists who only play when no one else is around. They're the ones you've heard are great singers, but you've never really heard them sing. They're the great debaters, actors, and math geniuses who live out their passions with excellence, but only in the safety of their bedrooms. Hidden passion eventually dies like a plant without sunlight. If you're confining what you love to the quietness of your room, stick your face into the world and let your family, friends, church, and everyone else see what you love doing. Live your passion with the boldness it deserves. If you're going to change the world with it, you have to actually be using it in the world.

Look for mentors.

Here's the thing about you and your passion—you're not the only one. Are you passionate about banking? There's a bank president in your town who probably wants someone she can invest in. Are you a singer? Do you love working with wood? Are you passionate about words? Your passion, whatever it is, is shared by someone else—and that someone is probably older, more experienced than you, and willing to invest in you. They're there to teach you what they've learned and help you up to the place they are with their passion. It could be your neighbor, your grandpop, or that crazy aunt who has 17 kittens living in her house. Or, you might need to search out someone you've never met. Make a few phone calls, search the Internet. This is your passion, and that person is part of your refining it. Find those folks, ask them to invest in you, and submit yourself to their teaching and direction. The more they mentor you, the clearer your passion and your ability to use it will become.

Ignore people who say you're too passionate.

You know those people who tell you to shut up, live quietly, and not infect other people with your desire to pursue your passion relentlessly? Tell them to take a walk. Those people who want you to live in the concrete jungle with the other monkeys? Put them on the B team. People who pull you away from your passion aren't looking out for your best interests. You're making them uncomfortable, and they don't like it. There are always going to be people who don't want you to live your passion because you remind them of their inability to live theirs. Your life makes them uncomfortable. So, go ahead, make them nervous. Live what you love. Who says they're right?

Remind people of the Source.

I don't mean you have to offer up a holier-than-everyone-else "Well, it's just God's power in me" response whenever anyone compliments your passion. Those overly psycho-spiritual responses just make you look silly. When people notice what you're good at, say, "Thanks." But if the conversation goes further, share a little bit about the journey you've been on to discover your passion. Tell them your belief about where it came from. Educate them on the difficulties you've had in pursuing it. Tell them you've prayed and offered who you are to God, and have asked him to use who you are. Tell them you're scared and you love that scared feeling. Tell them everything. Be honest. Follow the example of Paul, who always reminded folks that his passion for preaching the Good News of Christ wasn't his own doing: "I want you to know, brothers, that the gospel I preached is not something that man made up. I did not receive it from any man, nor was I taught it; rather, I received it by revelation from Jesus Christ (Galatians 1:11-12).

Do what you can to lead others' eyes back onto the presence of God in your life. That honesty is part of the footprint-leaving process. It tells people that you're not a superhuman who only eats once a week and never sleeps. It lets them know that you don't own what you love, yet you love it enough to make it yours. And it makes them want to live what they love, too.

FOLLOWING YOUR PASSION

I'm reminded fairly often, just by observing life, that passion is unavoidable. If you have it, it's an almost uncontrollable reaction to use it, as often as you breathe.

Every now and then, I'm lucky enough to get to teach at the university alongside some of the dreaming friends from my church. When I do, I often give my students a simple group project where they are stuck on a sinking boat with nineteen other people. There are all kinds of people on the boat: Businesspeople and homeless folks, athletes and couch potatoes, young and old, people with a wide variety of abilities and disabilities—a real cross-section of society. I tell them they've only got a single lifeboat that can hold only five people—and they have to choose which five get to live. It's not a comfortable assignment for students who take things too literally or who feel deeply about all things, even fake scenarios. And honestly, the assignment is intended to lead to a discussion about life and what actually gives life value.

These are primarily engineering students who spend time in their other classes building circuit boards, imagining new buildings and structures, programming in strange machine languages, and a host of other strange left-brained skills I can't even imagine. Just about every time I give the assignment, I'll have at least one group of passionate dreamers aching to put what they love into action. They want to break the rules and rethink the scenario, trying to find a way to save more people. It goes like this...

"Mr. Baker...can we use whatever we might be able to find on the sinking boat?"

"What do you mean?"

"Well, there would be wood and metal and things that float still connected to the bigger boat that we can use to save more people. Are we allowed to use those things?"

It frustrates them so badly that I force them to stay inside the box of the assignment. I have to contain their passion for rethinking, reshaping, and rewiring large objects; if I let them get too creative, they'll figure out how to save everyone, and we'll never get to the conversation that's the whole point of the exercise. But it kills me that I have to rein them in, and it's awfully frustrating to some students. They want me to give them the permission to think outside the box, to redesign the scenario. If I let them, they'd bring wood, metal, and a few other materials to the next class, ready to rebuild their lifeboats and put their passion into action.

You know, that's passion happening right there in my class. From the moment the scenario hits their desks, to the moment they're drawing up plans, to the moment where they create the new thing, their passion either comes out, almost uncontrollably—or they sit there frustrated that I won't let them think as far outside the box as they're wired to.

So, what about you? What do you have that uncontrollable, unbridled desire to spend your entire life doing? What do you love doing with your free time? What are you passionate about?

God has put that desire in you. Follow what he's put there, because it's there to help you impact the planet in your own unique way.

PUT YOUR FOOT DOWN

What passions has God placed within you? Take the next step by thinking through these questions on your own or talking them over with a friend.

- Name two things you're passionate about. What makes you feel these things are your passion?

- Who in your life is a living example of passion? What can you learn from that person?

- Whom can you invite into your life to help you perfect your passion?

- How can you shape the planet with your passion right now?

chapter 9

WHAT IF EXCELLENCE REALLY MATTERED...

...would you rise to the challenge?

I love movies. I'm a movie addict...a cinema junkie. Part of the deal with me and movies is, they are my white noise. I put movies on, pop headphones in my ears, and I can concentrate. The noise of the movie and the different things flashing on the screen are just enough distraction for me so I can focus myself in another direction. Before the days of downloadable and streaming movies, I was a frequent customer at the local Blockbuster. They knew me by my first name, and I never had to show my ID or membership card. Sometimes I even got my late fees comped.

I ran into one of my students while I was renting a video a few years back, and we had this interchange that still bothers me. We met in the comedy section, and he caught me up on his life since leaving my class...what he'd been up to, who he'd been dating, what his summer plans were. Probably the most typical kind of adult-to-student conversation you could have.

I asked, "So, how has school been? Are you keeping your head above the academic water? Staying afloat?"

"School's been okay. I'm doing pretty well with my grades, so that's good." I was glad to hear that. He's an average student, and I relate to that, being an average student myself. "I'm doing okay in everything except Calc 2," he added. "I'm really not doing well in that class."

When he mentioned Calc 2, I felt my head turn sideways just a bit, and the expression on my face was a lot like the way a dog looks when he hears a high-pitched whistle. Math and I don't have a very good relationship. I was really hoping he wouldn't try to explain why he wasn't doing well, or share examples of particular math problems he couldn't figure out. I'm certain if he had, my head would have spun backward on my neck.

"I think the prof hates me and is working hard to fail me out," he continued. "Besides, I don't need the class anyway. It's not in my major, so I really don't care that much."

"Right. I get that. But it does affect your GPA, right? So if you bomb the class, won't that still affect you?"

"Not really. In my major, and in the jobs that I'm trying to get, they only care about the GPA in my major. I don't really need to do well in that class. I just have to pass it so I don't have to repeat it."

When he said that, there was this visible fork in the road...I could almost see it ahead of him. I had the choice to go down one of two roads with him. I could float him an "Oh, that's cool" every now and then, and let him assume I was fine with what he was saying. Or, I could walk him down the second road. The one that would challenge him to see the importance of excellence in his life. The one that would help him see he should never just give up or settle for a low grade in anything. I could have helped him see that it didn't matter whether or not that grade would affect his GPA, his bank account, or his relationships. It's important to strive and push for excellence, especially in one's weak areas.

I totally blew it. I walked with him down the easy road. I chose the path of non-confrontation and no discipleship, the one where he'd feel affirmed in his decision to lowball himself.

That moment has bothered me ever since. Is it really possible to change someone's mind in a video store? Could I have made a difference? Honestly, I'm not even sure I had credibility to ask the question I felt he needed to hear or to encourage him in the direction I wanted. I'm not the super-duper-A-student, not the kind of person who has the intellectual track record required to encourage others to do their best in their own academic careers.

I guess the bigger question I'm asking is: How does excellence affect the way we impact the world? Does excellence even matter? Is it really important to be a person who strives to be better in every area of life? Does that matter to God? Does it matter to others? And if it doesn't matter to others, should it?

GETTING BY IS NOT ENOUGH

Before I say what I'm about to say, I feel like I know your response. You (the reader, probably young-ish) will say that I (the writer, likely older than you) have no idea what I'm talking about, that I'm too old, or that I don't understand current student culture.

Well, whatever—here goes. Look gang, if you're going to take on this world and seek to change the world, whether it's for God or for yourself, you're going to have to step things up a bit. You're going to have to adopt an attitude that doesn't care much about your friends' opinions, the money you can make, or much of anything else. You're going to have to set your personal bar high—higher than others want you to set it, higher than others expect. You're going to have to work hard at leaping every obstacle you encounter. You're going to have to seek to become the best in your field. You're going to have to seek not just gradual change, but a total revision of current culture. You're going to have to rescue the world from where it is now, and the only way you're going to do that is if you decide to live a life of total commitment. Not normal. Not average. Not just enough to get all of us by...you're going to have to live for change.

From where I work, as a teacher, youthworker, and writer, I see students who seem totally conflicted about their roles on the planet. On one hand, I see students who desperately want to change the world. Some of them really want to help shape the world into a better place. They want to get involved. I love that.

On the other hand, I see students who believe strongly in the idea of entitlement. They believe they *deserve* a good life, plenty of money, and even fame, but they're not committed to work for any of that. They think they deserve a good life because they're American, or because they've earned it. Now if that's not you, then great. But I believe that you (person ready to begin the Work For Change movement) are in the minority.

When I look into the eyes of many of the students I teach, I don't see many who have an interest in making a selfless difference. Instead of students interested in changing the world, I see students interested in change-for-themselves—students who want a better job so they can buy bigger speakers, faster computers, prettier cars, or more gaming systems. I meet students who choose majors because they'll make a lot of money, not because they want to make a difference.

So I'm calling you out. I'm calling me out, too. I'm calling on all of us to strive for excellence in all that we do. We need to be committed to lives of excellence. Not because God will love us more. Not so we can receive more honors or find the fast track to heaven. We need to live with excellence because that's the most effective way to leave a footprint on the world. It's the best way to impact the world. Can you live excellently in each of these four areas?

Spiritual excellence

As I mentioned earlier, one of my jobs is teaching the Bible to college freshmen and sophomores. I teach at a university where students come from all over the globe to study all kind of disciplines. It's a Christian university—so most of the students who come here grew up in youth groups taught by youth pastors, probably attended an endless series of Bible studies and Sunday school classes, and sat through dozens of youth pastor Bible lectures. It's my job to teach about the Bible, but also turn students on to the content and beauty of God's Word. I'd like them to grasp the deep theology and beautiful imagery of Scripture. But over the years, it's become an exasperating quest to be as exciting as the whiz-bang youth ministries many of them are used to. Many of my students seem totally bored with the Bible. They feel they already know everything they need to know—

they've heard most of the stories and they understand the basics of the New Testament theologies. If they're interested in anything, it's Revelation...*everyone* wants to study Revelation because there's something there, but they don't know what. They like prophecy too, because while it's difficult to follow, it's weird and mystical. Other than that, they're really not interested.

Each year Christian publishers print and sell millions of Bibles. There are different Bibles designed for recovering addicts, retired people, student leaders, armchair archaeologists, newlyweds, and loads of others. Does that bother you? It bothers me. Instead of the transforming, liberating Word of God, we've reduced the Bible to a marketing project. There are loads of books like this one, attempting to help you with your spiritual life, walk with God, or some other deeper issue. There are tons of youth retreats, conventions, and Bible studies pushing students to live for God. But the problem is that we often settle for a diet spirituality that nibbles on God in private yet offers no real power to change the way we think, act, and work.

If all of our efforts were really impacting the world, we'd feel it more. We'd see more people becoming Christians. There would be more effective media organizations, not only in preaching the gospel but also in countering current media trends. Christian groups would be doing more than just yelling against internet porn, abortion, stem cell research, illegal music, and movie downloading...they'd be seeking to infect those issues with the truth of Scripture in a loving way.

I know—it's not your fault that Christianity is where it is. But what if it became your desire to rescue Jesus from the grip of the slick marketing campaign that Jesus and his truth have become locked inside? What if all the adults looked to you to fix what many of us have broken?

We need spiritual excellence, a belief in God that helps us rise above the climate we're stuck in, and one that desires pure authenticity before him. What would happen if you took up the challenge to love God passionately and honestly? What if we all dropped the trite

Christianese sayings, the silly T-shirt slogan Christianity, and our desire to build empires with our churches and simply loved every person we met, with the full extent of who we are? What would happen if we said to our churches "no more," and challenged the way they spend the money we tithe, challenged the staff they hire, challenged the ineffective ministries?

You know, this change could really happen if you and your generation took up the challenge to change the spiritual climate. Will you?

Academic excellence

Academically, we're in trouble.

I know, you immediately want to say, "Ah, the old dude has lost his mind. Schools are doing great..." If you were to say that, you'd be seriously wrong. Recent statistics show that cheating and plagiarism have grown increasingly common in U.S. high schools and universities. According to the Center for Academic Integrity, a recent study of more that 18,000 students at 61 U.S. public and parochial high schools found that 70 percent of respondents admitted to one or more instances of serious cheating on a test. Over 60 percent of the students in that study admitted to some form of plagiarism, and half of all students said they'd used the Internet to engage in some form of plagiarism. In another survey cited by *U.S. News and World Report*, 75 percent of college students admitted to cheating, and nearly 85 percent of college students said cheating was "necessary" to get ahead.

Stop and ask yourself, why do more than half of all college and high school students choose to cheat? Why do so many submitted academic papers include material copied off the Web? It's not because academics haven't kept up with culture and technology. It's because we've lowered our standards and have equated cheating with borrowing. We've spent very little time teaching students the ethics that run like an electric current through the subjects taught.

But academic excellence is more than that. It's frustrating that so many universities still embrace an archaic model of education, continuing to teach solely via lectures to students seated in chairs and rows. (I'm guilty of this myself—I rely on lecture too much when I teach.) What about a creative approach to education that immerses students in the subject through active learning, doing projects, role playing, art, and drama? Why do we settle for old models that have been proven ineffective? It's no wonder many students lack enthusiasm.

Academia needs you to be enthusiastic about what you're studying. We need you to respectfully challenge your teacher's thinking. We need you to push for more creativity, asking your teachers to teach to your learning style. We need you to set the bar high, and learn more than you need to pass the test, read more than you're assigned, and work with more excellence than is needed to get by. Academia needs people—people like you—to get their degrees, reach inside it, and transform it into a system that fosters genuine learning.

What would happen to our world if more students took up the charge to become culture-shaping thinkers who seek to change society from the top down, from big institution to small college? What would happen if you rose above the current level of academic un-excellence, got your degree, and committed to help reshape the learning process in America? How big would your footprint be?

Professional excellence

I've met a ton of people who tell me writing is easy, and who say they have a book "right up here" (tapping their forehead) that is "all written, just waiting to come out." But writing isn't easy, at least for me. Working by yourself all the time is lonely, finding the right words is a struggle, and it's impossible to explain to people what you do. "I sit and write all day" doesn't sound very, uh, normal.

Expectations are huge. If your friends know you're a writer, they want to read what you've written. Family does, too. Your publisher has huge expectations, too. Yeah, they want to know what your ideas are, but they also want to know how your previous books have sold, because if you haven't sold a lot in the past, it's a bit of an uphill climb for you to sell more. And deadlines, sheesh. Editors and publishers set them and expect you to keep them. Attempt to bend them and you'll soon get an email or phone call wanting clarification and stressing why those dates are set in stone and must be met. And once the thing prints there's marketing, interviews, free books to family eagerly waiting to see what you say. And, of course, emails from people who love what you said, and emails from people who hate you for what you said.

There's a ton of pressure—but I love what God does in me in the process of writing. And I love that there's a bar I have to hurdle with every project. I enjoy seeing the goal, knowing it's set incredibly high, and then working my hardest to achieve it. It seems to me there are few professional goals that encourage workers to strive for excellence for its own sake. Instead of finding joy in doing a job, we find joy in getting a monetary reward or promotion. The goals are all selfish ones.

But that's not the way things should be. We should be committed to excellently doing our jobs because we're motivated just to be excellent. And, as Christians, we should be passionate about impacting our world through our occupation. And we do that by dropping our desire to be boldly obnoxious about the gospel and taking up the mantle of professional excellence. We have to reach into areas where Christians don't typically reach, doing things Christians don't typically do, offering our message in ways Christians don't typically offer. Why aren't there...

...more *politicians* who love their country and also love God, who are lovers of history, and who seek the best for all people—especially those who are most vulnerable?

...more *musicians* who are committed to creating high quality music, without feeling the need to pigeonhole themselves into categories like "Christian" so they can be marketed to the church demographic?

...more *writers* rooted in a committed faith who write culture-shaping books that don't have to do with politics, Christian self-help, or theology? Can't Christians write good stories that reach all of the book-buying public? Don't we have anything more to say other than "Jesus loves you, and your life will be perfect if you know him"?

...more *journalists* working for national networks who are also Christians, and reasonable thinkers who are able to offer a healthy, balanced perspective on values that honor God and also honor their Democratic, Republican, or Independent beliefs?

...more *businesspeople* who live out a Christian ethic, using their positions of power and influence to help the homeless and forgotten in society?

Why aren't there more Christians who think it's more important to have their work reveal Jesus' values rather than their T-shirts reveal Jesus slogans? Why can't we be people whose faith makes a difference in the way we do our jobs, and not people who seek to be different in our rhetoric, but not our performance? What would happen if we decided that we would change culture by loving what we did for money, and used that to change society?

Personal excellence

Right now, too many culture-shaping leaders are making really bad decisions. And we're making that possible, by voting them into office, by encouraging them with our dollars, and by letting them preach their revised morality at us. Right now...

...There are athletes getting busted repeatedly for steroid use. Some have loudly proclaimed they didn't use, and then we found out not only that they did use steroids but also that they were liars.

...There are politicians who talk a lot about moral integrity getting busted for sex scandals. One had an inappropriate IM conversation with a coworker. Another, a mayor, admitted having sex with prostitutes. When people get caught doing that stuff, they always come on TV with great apologies—but are they sorry for what they've done or just sorry that they got caught?

...There are Wall Street financial gurus getting caught pilfering company accounts and using the money to buy themselves expensive toys.

...There are singers parading around in skimpy outfits whose lives send the message that young girls need to show lots of skin if they want to be popular. They may be making excellent music, but what kind of influence are they having?

...There are news reports about older men whose houses are raided, and the police find evidence that they've been holding women as sex slaves or running their own child pornography rings.

The point is that what we do in private, the way we act when we think no one is looking, makes a world of difference in who we are. What you do in secret defines your character and shapes who you are.

I know a guy who has been stuck in an addiction to Internet pornography. He'd surf the Web in search of it every chance he could get. He surfed at work, at home. He bought it. He rented it. His wife caught him several times and each time they discussed it and he swore he'd never do it again. He told her he didn't want this to affect their relationship, and she said it wouldn't, as long as he stopped.

But he didn't stop. And the gulf between them grew and grew. Before long they were as close as Europe is to Mexico. They divorced and their kids got caught in an uncomfortable situation. The wife struggled to explain their divorce to her friends. The porn was destroying his life—and he kept right on surfing.

I know...I chose one of those extreme situations, one that'll both gross you out and make you feel angry. I bet you've got stories from your life just like that one, where someone you know got caught in public for something they never thought anyone would discover.

I'm imperfect, but I want to believe my life in God isn't just about never getting caught. Our life shouldn't be about hiding things, it should be about openness. That's one of the things about sin—it forces us to keep crazy secrets from people who love us. Forget the fact that God sees everything we do for just a moment. What about the importance of living a life that honors God with everything we are, including the uncomfortable corners, the difficult temptations, and the areas where we've struggled and failed?

We don't have to earn God's love for us—but we do have to live up to it. Imagine God's love as a very tall fence, one that all of us are challenged, from the day we are born, to climb. Our entire life is spent on that fence climbing and climbing, and loving the effort. And our only real accomplishment in life is to get to the top of that fence. We can spend our lives at the bottom of that fence, looking up, loving how it looks, but never surrendering ourselves to the journey to the top. We can spend our lives stuck in the middle of the journey, halfway to total and complete love, but only halfway, keeping an eye on what's below, what we left behind. Or, we can rise to the challenge and commit every move up the fence to God, promising ourselves that we will get to the top and live up to the love that God has for us.

What would happen to your world if you committed yourself to living a life of personal excellence? Whom would you infect? What would change?

CHANGING THE PLANET WITH YOUR EXCELLENCE

Excellence attracts people. The more we fill our lives with excellence, the more people will want to be around us. The more we live out excellence, the bigger difference we'll make in the world. Your work will be changed by your commitment to excellence. You friends will be changed. Your family, your church, your personal life...everything will be changed.

Set your standards high, live up to them, let others see your success and failure, and people will be influenced. What kind of strategies can help us do this?

Live by Scripture.

I'm not saying we need to read the Bible more. I'm saying we need to actively live what the Bible says. We need to immerse ourselves in the truth of Scripture and then embody what we've found there. The call to raise our lives up to the calling of Christ is replete throughout Scripture, but Paul outlines it very well here:

> As a prisoner for the Lord, then, I urge you to live a life worthy of the calling you have received. Be completely humble and gentle; be patient, bearing with one another in love. Make every effort to keep the unity of the Spirit through the bond of peace. (Ephesians 4:1-3)

Our call is to live in faithful response to the love of God. What we do with our lives is a living testimony, a statement of our commitment to the truth of God's love and our constant struggle to remain consistent with that truth.

What would happen in your life if those around you saw you living the truth you read about on Sundays?

Take advantage of each day.

I know an average student who gets up early every day, reads his Bible, takes a shower, studies for a bit, and then goes to breakfast. He's smart, but he's not the smartest guy you've ever met. He's popular, but he's not the Big Man On Campus. Yet, he's found favor with many of his professors. He's about to graduate college and has several businesses begging him to accept their offers. What's so attractive about this guy? It's very simple: He takes advantage of time. He doesn't waste any of it. Not only is his life a good example for any of us looking for a way to get the most out of our day, it's a great example of living with excellence. If he's living that way now, he'll live that way as he gets older. Imagine what he will accomplish each day.

What would happen in your life if you got out of bed 60 minutes earlier every day? What could you accomplish?

Keep your commitments.

I recently had a discussion with one of my kids that brought this home to me. She's in a school play, and it's getting difficult. The demands on her time are huge—there's school to study for, lines to learn, songs to remember, dancing and blocking to commit to memory, friends to hang out with. She's overloaded. We were talking in the car and she asked, "Everything is piling on me, I can't take it. I want out. Can I quit the play, please?"

I wanted to say, "Yeah, sweetheart. I hear the pressure you're feeling. I'll go get the phone and call the director." But I didn't. The dad in me wanted to take over, but she'd made a promise. So instead, we talked about what it means to make a promise, to commit yourself to someone or something, and to stick with that commitment. Ultimately, she stayed in the play, and she did a wonderful job balancing her crazy schedule.

I don't want to sound corny, but the world needs promise keepers. The world needs people who are willing to stand by what they say they'll do.

What would happen to our planet if everyone kept their promises and stayed committed to what they said they'd do?

Set a vision and work to achieve it.

When one of my good friends was in college, he set a goal of getting a job at a national bank when he graduated, one that influences all the other banks in America. Because he prepared in college, got good grades, and had the right experience, he easily landed that job. When he got it, he set another vision...to get his MBA and use his banking experience to get a management job at a large company. He got his MBA and got a job in lower management at a large store, but that wasn't enough for him. So he slowly moved up to upper management, not through cutting corners, demanding promotions, or undercutting his coworkers. He arrived early every day, worked hard when he was there, took advantage of opportunities, and impressed his bosses. He did his work with excellence.

You know, we've overblown the concept of vision—made it this big business term and fluffed it up with language that's only used by high-powered corporate executives. But vision is really quite simple: It's just setting a very big goal, a life-encompassing one, and then working your hardest to achieve it. Sometimes God shows us very clearly what that vision is. Other times, we set it. But either way, we have to work to reach it—that's the difficult part.

What would happen in your life and the lives around you if you publicly set a goal and then publicly worked hard at meeting that goal? What if you didn't meet that goal, but openly talked about how it felt to try to reach it, and then openly talked about how it felt to not meet that goal?

Do your best, no matter what.

Remember that teacher who made you so angry in grade school? She always yelled at you and never gave you the grade you deserved. Remember how you felt like she was out to get you? What did you want to do? I can tell you exactly what I wanted to do when I had a teacher like that: I wanted to give up. I wanted to hurt her feelings by doing my worst. I hoped that maybe if she saw I was doing badly, she'd ease up on me, and she and I would eventually be cool (and my grade would climb up out of the sewer).

The hardest part of doing our best is the whole "no matter what" part. We face opposition every day, don't we? Do you ever feel like people are out to get you, to make fun of your best efforts, and to diminish every accomplishment you have?

What would happen if you viewed every obstacle or opponent as an opportunity to prove you will not be beaten, can't be kicked off track, and won't give up on your dream?

Work hard to be an influence.

A few weeks ago I was in a party store, which is a dangerous place for me. I have a strange attraction to fake severed body parts, multi-colored wigs, silly hats, plastic vomit, rubber snot, and, most of all, fake poo. That day, I stumbled across the most perfect replica of human poo. I bought it and even called a few friends on the way home to brag. I waited about four days, then placed in on the toilet seat at home and waited for someone to discover it. To make a long, wonderful, fantastic story short, my son found it, tried to clean the seat off (thinking that maybe he'd made the mistake), got grossed out, called everyone in, and we all had a very long laugh.

I hadn't really thought about what the incident would do to my kids. But my little fake poo joke gave my kids permission to do the same thing to me. They talked their Meemaw into taking them to the same party store, and then they went crazy buying all kinds of pranks to play on me. As of today, I have been electrocuted by a fake cell phone, stepped in fake dog poo, nearly slipped on plastic vomit, ingested sneezing powder on a brownie, and nearly lost my mind when I saw a bear-claw scratch on the back of our minivan. And, I'm told that the pranks aren't done, and I should be very, very worried. (Wait until they find out that I also bought sour gum, fake roaches, and a few other gags.)

The moral of the story is: Think about how you live, because you can be sure others will imitate you. And that's especially true if you live with excellence. Excellence is contagious. Our desire to be our best will infect others with a desire to be their best. We might not be leaving fake poo hoping others will catch the wind of our enthusiasm (ew!), but by demonstrating a passion for God, a commitment to academic integrity, a love for our jobs, and a commitment to personal integrity—in short, a life of excellence—we will influence the people around us.

CLIMB THE HILL

I need to confess that writing this chapter has been a convicting experience for me. I've struggled with each sentence I've typed. I've included this topic because I know it's important, and I've pointed fingers at others who struggle with excellence in order to help make my points relatable. But, to be honest, this is the part of leaving a footprint that I struggle with the most in my own life. I don't live with excellence with any consistency. There are days, even weeks, when I'm a total slouch. And, there are some pretty important areas of my own life that I neglect far too often. If we were to meet, you might decide I need to read this chapter more than you do. But maybe that's why I think this is such an important topic as we consider how exactly we will shape the planet, because I know that it's been a huge struggle in my own life.

In many ways, excellence is really a spiritual issue, and one that's been around for a long time. Our struggle is as old as Paul's words where he says, "I know that good itself does not dwell in me, that is, in my sinful nature. For I have the desire to do what is good, but I cannot carry it out. For I do not do the good I want to do, but the evil I do not want to do—this I keep on doing" (Romans 7:18-19). Could it be that the challenge of living with excellence is as old as the Adam and Eve story, and all of this is *their* fault?

But this isn't about finding someone to blame or diffusing our inabilities by over-spiritualizing our own lack of integrity. As I've reflected on my life, I've discovered it's about owning up to, accepting, and taking charge of the areas of life where I've messed up. I don't know exactly what that means for you, because I believe the struggle for personal excellence is as unique as a fingerprint. But for me, living excellently means being honest about things in my own life, and working hard to change areas where I'm not who I want to be. It means hard conversations with myself and with others, taking charge of the mistakes, asking God to continue shaping me into the person he wants me to be. That's the ownership process, I think—

seeing, surrendering, changing, and remembering. The more I read Paul's letters in the New Testament, that seems to be the way he thought of it, too.

Excellence is the hill that stands in the distance before us, the one you know you have to hike up as a part of the journey. And sometimes we find ourselves standing at the foot of that hill, trying to psych ourselves up, and maybe wishing there was some way around it. "Oh, wow. Really? *This* hill? Okay, no, really?"

That's where I am. I hope you're there at the base with me, ready to climb that hill, because the world truly needs God-fearing people who live with excellence. It's part of our striving toward godliness, and the strongest way to leave a lasting footprint.

PUT YOUR FOOT DOWN
Do you struggle to live with excellence? Take the next step by thinking through these questions on your own or talking them over with a friend.

- With which areas of excellence do you struggle most?

- In which areas of excellence are you doing a good job?

- Who in your life is an example of excellence? What can you learn from them?

- What would have to change in your life for you to live "excellently"?

chapter 10

WHAT IF YOU COULD LIVE
LIKE A TRAVELER...

...would you shed your ordinary, tourist self?

When I surrendered my life to Christ, I soon found myself treading water in a deep pool of "do nots." The version of Christianity I was taught as a teenager focused mostly on a long list of things Christians weren't supposed to do. Dancing got you pregnant, short shorts led to sex, and men who wore their hair long were rebelling against God. We were told most popular movies were birthed within the church of Satan, and that any kind of music with a beat was probably hand-delivered to our houses by the devil himself. As kids in youth group, we attended seminars where adults spent hours spinning records backward for us, helping us hear garbled messages they believed were laced into the songs, and convincing us that record companies had special rooms where they prayed demons into their records and tapes. Listening to AC/DC would make you bisexual, and jamming to KISS told the world you really were a "Knight In Satan's Service." Acoustic guitars could honor Jesus, but electric guitars were a sign that you'd sold your soul to Beelzebub. Being a Christian meant memorizing as much of the Bible as possible so you could argue it with that other Christian kid up the street.

My Christian college experience was the same, filled with tons of "do nots." Good Christian girls always wore dresses and never walked on the side of the street where the boys' dorm was. Good Christian boys wore shirts with collars and kept their hair cut short and neatly combed. And, even though I graduated six years after I became a Christian, girls were still getting pregnant from dancing. Hadn't they found a way to prevent that yet?

Popular Christianity is too often ruled by pointless, silly, and empty rules. We spend so much time focused on should nots, can nots, and better nots that we end up never really experiencing anything. Maybe we set up these strict rules because we want some way of measuring whether we're really holy. Maybe we fear that the "do nots" in God's Ten Commandments don't quite cover all the bases, so we think we need to create a few more lists of our own. But our desire to fill our lives with lists of limitations affects both our passion and our ability to shape the world the way God planned us to shape it.

Imagine a baby taking its first steps, only to have one of its parents standing next to it with a ruler. Each step the baby attempts, the parent slaps its feet and lets out a stern "No!" That's the way a lot of us imagine living for God. We hear God's call to step out, but then something slaps us back—either an old family rule, an ancient edict, or our own fears. The result is a lot of believers who have all the courage they need in God, but none of it in themselves. These Christians stay packed away safely in churches, reading through their do-not lists, but never really impacting the world around them.

You know, it's possible for us to live our entire lives without ever really making a difference, walking from garage-sale spirituality to prepackaged answer to just-add-water theology. But then we wake up ten years later and realize we've spent our days without any real purpose, having never really lived. Do you want to live your life in God like that? I don't.

So, you've got a choice before you. You can stay inside the safety of the tour bus and watch the world through the windows. You can continue to live your Christian life like a tourist, sightseeing your way through Christianity. Or you can get out and live as God intended, as a traveler, seeking to experience everything God has for you. You can live as someone who's hungry to discover new things, and, in turn, impact the planet the way God intended.

TRAVELERS LIVE *PASSIONATELY*

Each year, at least one of my kids is involved in some kind of bug project at school. In order to learn all they need to know about bugs, how they work and what they're made of, the kids are required to gather, mount, and label different kinds of insects. One year, my kids scored a few scorpions that they kept in a mayonnaise jar on top of the fridge. Those scorpions lived in that jar atop the fridge for several days, eating the tiny pieces of lettuce my kids put in the jar for them. Each night, those nocturnal stingy-beasts would stand at attention... their tails wrapped up close to them, ready to attack. But during the day, they'd lie around like two innocent couch potatoes.

Those two little guys spent their days in that little jar unable to touch or be touched by the outside world and, to tell you the truth, they were dead for about a week before we noticed. When my daughter finally opened the jar, a horrible stink filled the room. These dead scorpions, and the mounds of lettuce we'd put in for them, stank so very badly.

Imagine...your entire life lived inside the protection of a glass jar where nothing touches you or affects you or challenges you. How long can you really live that way before you start to stink? Does that sound like living?

Travelers get outside the jar and go to unexplored places. They live in the deserts with people in need. They eat local food. They respect the safe, secure, and protected, but they do not long to live safely, securely, or protected. They understand that the world is too beautiful to experience from inside the jar. Unlike tourists, whose feet carry them only on the most well-trodden paths, you'll notice travelers' footprints when you're exploring caves you thought no one had discovered.

Safe ought to be our enemy. Safe tells us that the typical is best, and discovery is better sitting and eating rather than walking and learning. If you want to passionately pursue impacting the planet, you have to live outside the boundary of the safe. Can you do that?

TRAVELERS CELEBRATE *UNIQUENESS*

Remember that old Dr. Seuss story about the Sneeches—those goofy looking animals with tiny heads and huge bottoms who wanted so desperately to all be alike? Some of them had stars on their bellies, and so the plain-bellied ones started getting stars put on so they'd look more like the star-bellies. In the meantime, some of the star-bellies were getting their stars removed to look like the plain-bellied ones. Everyone was busy trying to look like everyone else.

Does that seem ridiculous? What if we all spoke the same way, followed the same rules, wore the same clothes, and thought the same way about everything—politically, socially, and spiritually? What if we were all supposed to listen to the same music, read the same books, watch the same television shows, vote for the same president, work for the same causes, and use identical language to describe how we felt about all of that. Sounds crazy, huh? Sadly, I think that describes most of the Christian community in America. We're not as diverse as we think we are.

Marketing feeds on this mentality. We're told we'll be happier if we buy certain clothes or drive a certain car. And we're sold spirituality the same way. We're told that if we embrace Jesus, we'll have the lives *like other Christians*. But I don't think God wants us all to be predictable cookie-cutter imitations of each other. When that happens, our passion is killed and our ability to hear God's voice calling us to the unique life he has in store for us is lost. God did not love us into existence so we could fall backward into boring sameness. God created us as travelers—each of us designed to follow a unique path that is ours alone. But the world makes us into tourists.

TRAVELERS *DREAM*

You've probably never heard of the amazing magician, the Great Morrisini. That's because the skilled illusionist once met up with a jerk who discouraged him into resigning from the performing arts. I loved performing illusions when I was young. I'd set up anywhere...birthday parties, family dinners, street corners, public bathrooms...I didn't care. My parents took me to magic shops and loaned me money to buy all kinds of cool props and tricks. I had business cards made that read "The Great Morrisini," (at the time, the only good use for my middle name, Morris) complete with my phone number.

One night, a friend of my parents asked me, "So, Tim, what do you think you'll do with your life?" I responded, "I want to be a magician, and I'm pretty good at it." To which the un-dreamer responded, "Yeah, well, that'll change seven times before you get to be my age..." That dude was a total tourist. But I took his words to heart—and eventually packed up my tricks and forgot about magic. My dream of being a world-famous illusionist was murdered.

Tourists don't understand dreaming. They cannot grasp—physically, emotionally, or psychologically—the gravity and importance of The Dream. They may tolerate a little talk about dreams, but usually they'll respond with some perfectly crafted negative comment, intended to ruin the traveler's focus and drain his positive outlook with a vampirish swoop. Try dreaming in the presence of a tourist and you'll get a polite pat on the head, a gentle condescending grin, and then you'll be totally ignored.

Dreaming moved Gutenberg to create the printing press, guided Newton to invent the telescope, and inspired the Montgolfier brothers to craft the hot air balloon. Dreamers are the travelers that leave footprints. Travelers seek out wise people, hunt for clues. When they don't uncover everything they're searching for, they keep searching. If they created their own T-shirts, they'd print "Hungry" on them. If they even cared about labeling their lives, they'd label them "Searching." Travelers are the reason people put up "No Trespassing" signs.

TRAVELERS ARE "UN-PERFECT"

I'm the son of an artist. I grew up appreciating that a shapeless lump of clay could be crafted into something both useful and beautiful and that a blank canvas would one day be the home of a wonderful work of art. I grew up amidst sketchbooks filled with pencil drawings and poems, went to quite a few art festivals and fairs, and walked through my share of museums. And my experience is that many people tend to think that the more *perfect* a work of art is, the more *value* it has. It might not be perfect in the mind of the artist, but once someone considers a work perfect, and, perfect above all other works, it gains value—in some cases a great deal of value.

But this connection between value and perfection has really messed us up. It has made us think that we need to be perfect in order to be valuable. We spend our lives trying to measure up to some media-created ideal of perfection before we can believe we are *valuable*. Everything in our lives has to hit some idealistic bull's-eye, and if we're not able to hit that target, we get depressed, we give up, or worse, we don't even try. We figure that if God were *really* in our corner and calling us to whatever we're trying to do, then we'd be successful. Because, you know...if God loves you, you'll be the best at whatever you try—right? God is found only in the perfect and the beautiful and the wonderfully put together. He'd never inhabit a life less than perfect, an occupation less than holy, a sub-4.0 GPA. God does not love the wandering ugly person who seems to fail more often than she succeeds.

But you know, that is total tourist thinking.

The traveler embraces her holy imperfection. She doesn't admire perfection or long for it. She loathes the idea of having arrived at something. Arrived people are not hungry people, and the traveler stays hungry. She realizes that perfection is a process toward God, guided by God, interested only in God. The traveler embraces the unconditional love of God as the song of her life, and she sings that song over and over in her soul.

TRAVELERS AREN'T LIMITED BY *MAPS*

I've lived in the same town for ten years, and I still need help finding my way at times. I seem to make a wrong turn just about every time

I drive somewhere—heading left when I ought to go right, or vice versa. When you're challenged in this area, it can really help to have a map. But I'm a bit frustrated in that area, too. I can't read city maps very well, either, and I definitely struggle to keep it all going—driving and reading the map and thinking all at the same time.

I know maps are important, but who says we're supposed to live our lives by a map someone else has created? Somewhere along the way, many of us picked up the idea that we're supposed to live by the map instead of living the map. We think we're supposed to adopt the map as the director of our lives, instead of taking a blank paper along with us, and mapping life as we live it.

Let's say you map out a forest—where each boulder and tree and stream is. That map is static—once it's complete, it never changes. But life isn't static. The terrain of our lives is dynamic—it is constantly changing, refining, and new territory is being discovered. Tourists live by the static map...their lives married to the certainty of the predetermined chart. Travelers look forward to the opportunity to chart new territory. They seek out what's new, they long for the unexplored, uncharted territory. The dynamic map matches the dynamic, always changing life of the traveler.

TRAVELERS UNDERSTAND *TRANSFORMATION*

Travelers realize that, as God is making us, everything is changing. They live their lives in constant transition, and not with a feeling of having arrived. They recognize that we are all on a common journey, and that we've not yet reached the destination God has in mind.

And because travelers are in transition all the time, they make mistakes. They live in danger of stepping on the toes of the established thinking. When you read the accounts of the apostles in the New Testament, you read about people who loved God so much that they embraced transition and transformation regardless of the cost. And because of that, many people sought to label, deny, and lie about them—like here, where a lawyer named Tertullus is talking about the apostle Paul...

> "We have found this man to be a troublemaker, stirring
> up riots among the Jews all over the world. He is a ring-
> leader of the Nazarene sect and even tried to desecrate
> the temple; so we seized him. By examining him yourself
> you will be able to learn the truth about all these charges
> we are bringing against him." (Acts 24:5-8)

You don't get people saying that stuff about you because you love the tourist bus. Paul later says that Tertullus wasn't being totally truthful, but it's quite possible that riots were springing up whenever Paul came to town, and that the Jewish officials felt like Paul was desecrating the temple somehow. But the reason for the uproar wasn't the character of Paul, but his passion for sharing the radical, life-transforming message of Christ.

Being a traveler means never settling for the easy, prepackaged pabulum of bumper sticker variety Christianity. The only way to traveler living is submitting everything to God and allowing him to continue transforming our souls. The tourist Christian *has been changed*, but the traveler Christian *is being changed*. Travelers recognize that when Paul says, "Work out your salvation with fear and trembling" (Philippians 2:12), he's talking about a process that's ongoing. When some people quote that verse, they think it means we need to agree on every issue. But working out your salvation means being willing to take God's leading seriously, and talking about the things we don't agree about. It means thinking about things some people might call heretical. It means that our salvation, God's saving work in our lives, is far too important to be bottled up in something neat, perfect, and tidy.

Quit striving to be just like everyone else and enjoy who you are, how you were made, and the unique difference God wants to make through you. If you're caught up in thinking life is about trying to hit some perfect target, try embracing your unusual self, your awkward side. God doesn't always work in the perfect. In fact, I think he works most often in the imperfect.

It's easier to let our lives be ruled by "do nots," isn't it? Wouldn't it be easier to stay in the rest of the group, observing the world but never daring to experience it? Maybe it's easier, but it's not the way God wants us to live. When I die, I don't want people to say, "Wow, he was so...normal and typical. He did such a good job making sure the system kept working." I want them to say that I challenged things, that I grasped who I was so confidently, that breaking away from established thinking was easy. I want them to use words like *dreamer* and *exciting*. I want them to laugh at the mistakes I made, but also to remember with total amazement all that God was able to accomplish through me. And that won't happen, for me or for you, if we just play it safe, follow the rules, and let others decide who we are.

CHANGING THE PLANET BY TRAVELING THROUGH IT

Living as a traveler means stepping outside the safe and secure and journeying into the better life God has in store for you. Will you do that? There's so much waiting to be challenged and changed. There's so much for you to experience. But you have to decide that you are willing to step away from what you're used to, and allow God to lead you onto the path that leads to challenges and insecurity. Are you ready to begin the journey?

If you're ready to move from where you are now and into the dangerous, exciting life of a traveler, try taking these steps...

Explore the place where you are now.

You don't have to hop a plane to some distant land to prove that you're a traveler. What about the places nearby that you've never explored—the back roads that lead into your city, the restaurants that look scary, the downtown area in the city 30 minutes away? There are unexplored places near you. Check them out. Take time to look around the places you've never noticed. How can you *love* where you live unless you *know* where you live? Go to a Wal-Mart or a strip mall at different times of the day and notice the people who shop there. Do the same thing at movie theaters, gas stations, emergency rooms. Visit your local library and the bookstores in your city. Sit in coffee shops and fast food places and study the people. And then, branch out...go to neighboring cities, and then go even further. Do your best to really *see* where you live.

Know the political happenings in your culture.

Who is the mayor of your city? What's happening in your state legislature? Who is your local representative? Do you know the positions of the political leaders in your city? Are you aware of the current list of bills being debated in Congress? Have you listened to one of the President's speeches lately? Being a traveler means being aware of what's happening in the political climate, knowing who's working for change and who's not, and understanding where your country, your state, and your local community are heading.

And please...I'm not saying you need to join a right- or left-wing political group and become a full-time political activist. You should know the political climate so you can think ahead with others, and see where you can work in a loving way to make the world a better place. You should know those things so you can best speak to your culture and love within it.

Have a global perspective.

Did you know there are TV shows similar to *American Idol* in 40 different countries? Did you know there's a movie industry in India that is just as powerful and influential as the one in Hollywood? If you live in the United States, get to know what is happening in Africa. If you live in Spain, get to know what is happening in the United States. Search Amazon.com to find out what books are selling best in other countries. Read newspapers from other countries to get the perspectives of the people there. Get to know people from other cultures... ask them to teach you how to cook something indigenous to their culture. There is a richness of expression that's found as we explore different cultures. Don't let your culture limit you.

Get a passport and use it.

Studying other cultures and parts of the world from afar is great, but there's no substitute for actually being there. There are important foods you've never eaten—try them in the culture they're cooked in. There are works of art native to every country—go and see them. There are smells in villages that can only be experienced by being there. Go and smell them. I'll never forget my first visit to a poverty-stricken city in Mexico. It's one thing to read about poverty or see poverty on television, but it something very different to see, smell, and feel the hunger of the people around you. Go places around the world and get out of your comfort zone. Don't go to preach the gospel or tell them what you know...go to learn, surrender yourself to the experience, and ask God to use it to shape who you are.

Team up with other travelers.

Consider the difference between "I" and "we." One person—one "I"—acting alone for change is not a revolution. In fact, one solitary person working for change often ends up tired, ineffective, and burned out. But a bunch of people, a bunch of "I's" working together as a "we" can make a huge difference. Consider the people you know who think like you, who share similar passions or beliefs, and find ways to join together and love the world into a different place. Find others like you, get together with them, and talk about your passion. If you can't find others who already feel like you do, go and make them.

Know technology.

I know...you use Facebook, you text your friends three states over, you comb Wikipedia researching your next paper, and you download tons of music and movies—but I'm not talking about that. I'm saying, *know* technology beyond the user level. Understand how the cyberworld works beyond knowing which button you need to push to bid for stuff on eBay. Grasp the intricacies of how Web pages are designed, understand digital copyrights...know that stuff so you can be on the front end of designing the next generation of technology.

Read. Watch movies. Listen to music. Watch television.
I know, I know...the media are evil and all that, but culture is shaped in those places we're often told to be careful with. Important thinking happens in books, important attitudes are expressed in songs, and movies are often the main conveyors of current spiritual thought. How can you really know what people are thinking if you live in a tiny Christian bubble? Can you really understand current thinking if you don't read a few books by non-Christians? Can you really grasp where the world is headed if you don't pay attention to what's happening in the media?

Seek out the places where you have influence.
You probably can't take over Wall Street (at least not tomorrow), but could you have a part in changing the quality of food served in your school cafeteria? You might not be able to speak directly to the President, but you can have a big influence on the officials in your city government. Think about the areas you might be able to influence in your immediate world and ask, "What can I do to effect change?" Don't just lend your support where change is already happening... create change. The best place to use your influence for change is a place where you are already invested. And, if you're not investing anywhere, today is the day to start.

Ask the magic "why?" about everything.
Change happens when people start asking questions. There is no

system, structure, idea, government, law, book, music, movie, or anything else that doesn't need someone to stand up and challenge it. The book you're holding right now began as an idea four years ago. I talked about it with several students, who helped me fill in some of the holes by asking many well-placed whys. It went before a publishing group who asked a few of their own whys. The cover was designed, debated, and redesigned. The manuscript was read, edited, challenged, revised, redreamed, re-edited, and rewritten several times (and this chapter was originally the third one in the book). In its final form, it will be read (or not read), talked about, questioned, and either panned or praised. People will ask "Why did he say that?" and "Why didn't he say this" over and over.

Asking why about everything you encounter is a good thing. Don't hesitate to toss them at your youth pastor, your teachers, and your friends; at the news; at your senators, congresspersons, and the president; at movies and books, at things that don't make sense.... everything. And, shoot, go ahead and toss a few dream-inspired why questions my way by emailing me at tim@timbaker.cc.

LET IT ALL GO

So, here we are, near the end of a conversation that's been going on for about 150 pages. But to be totally honest, I've struggled with these issues my entire life. I've wrestled with questions around my *calling* and *purpose* for as long as I can remember. There have been rare moments when I was certain I could clearly see God's hand working out his purpose in me. But there have been many more times when my search for God's plan felt more like looking for a match in a pitch-black cave. And, to be totally more-than-honest, despite my desire to be a traveler, there are times when I think I might be the biggest tourist that has ever lived.

I'm learning that this frustration is part of God's plan, too. I believe God wants us to be dissatisfied with the way things are, because our dissatisfaction opens us to the good stuff God seeks to grow in us.

Our discomfort with our present feeds our future. I believe God uses our frustration. In fact, that's part of what led me to want to write this book.

But knowing that God uses our frustration doesn't always help me. Throughout my life, as I've asked if I'm making a difference, leaving a dent, or helping to create meaning in my life or the lives of those I've touched, I haven't always been happy with the answers. I've looked into the mirror of my life, hoping to see great things in there, and yet, most often just seeing my own reflection—sometimes alone, sometimes with God in the background.

For the longest time, I've felt like I'm supposed to bring everything I've accumulated along with me on this journey. Not just who I am, but everything I've been told is true, everything I've created and built, everything I've ever believed—all the stuff I've picked up along the way. And there's part of me that still wants to cling to all those things, because they help me feel secure.

But when I look at the lives of the disciples, I don't see them clinging to what they've been in the past. In fact, I see them dropping everything to follow Jesus...

As Jesus walked beside the Sea of Galilee, he saw Simon and his brother Andrew casting a net into the lake, for they were fishermen. "Come, follow me," Jesus said, "and I will send you out to fish for people." At once they left their nets and followed him.

When he had gone a little farther, he saw James son of Zebedee and his brother John in a boat, preparing their nets. Without delay he called them, and they left their father Zebedee in the boat with the hired men and followed him. (Mark 1:16-20)

From what I can see, the disciples' lives were totally about shedding the things they'd once thought important for the cause of following Christ and, in turn, leaving a footprint others could see. And I think that's what God asks of us, too.

I recently read about a guy who'd lived through a fairly traumatic event and, faced with a very tough series of emotions and moments, he made an emotional-intellectual decision to make a big change in the way he'd been living. So you know what he did?

He put his entire life for sale on eBay.

Everything. Not just his house or his car. But also his furniture. His silverware and dishes. Rugs. Pictures. Books. Job. And I think he did it so he could let go of the past and launch out into his next big life adventure. When he talked about the future he was just beginning, he sounded like a prisoner freed from his chains. He's ready to take on the world without any of the extraneous stuff most of us "need" in order to survive.

Does that ring true to you? It does to me. I'm learning that a lot of life is about shedding what has been to make space for what is to come. Snakes shed skin, butterflies shed cocoons, cats shed fur, people shed extra weight, and jobs, and furniture...all in their search for something better. Shedding means change, a new part of life has begun, and without shedding that new life won't begin. Something has to be stripped away in order for the new to grow.

Letting go of the old isn't easy or painless, but if we're going to grow, it has to happen. Getting rid of old ideas, ones that don't fit you anymore, can sometimes be just as difficult as shedding your own skin. Can you forget all that you think you know about God, and open yourself to the change God wants to bring in and through you? Are you able to forget most of the human-theological ideas you've been taught? Are you willing to ditch the liturgy you were told was straight from God's mouth? Can you dump the rules your pastor said were "inspired," ignore what your friends say about what Christianity "really is," and jump into the huge, deep pool that is God, and let him recreate your traveler soul?

As painful as it can be, if you want to dent the planet, leave a footprint, change where you live or change just one life, you've got to be willing to get rid of a lot...maybe everything. You've got to let go of the things you thought were so very important, surrender them to God, let him take away what isn't essential, so you can be left with the stuff you most need in order to glorify him with your life.

PUT YOUR FOOT DOWN
Are you ready to live like a traveler? Take the next step by thinking through these questions on your own or talking them over with a friend.

- How are you participating in tourist living?

- Where do you feel you need to be stretched in your life? Whom can you invite into your life to stretch you?

- What aspects of your life prevent you from living with enthusiasm? What prevents you from "seeing the world"?

- What do you need to delete from your life to begin living like a traveler?

You'll laugh out loud at the embarrassing stories of Luke Lang, a self-proclaimed "freak of nature." While you're reading Luke's embarrassing stories—like the time he was beaten up by a girl in Karate class, or the time he was fighting for his life at Boy Scout camp—you'll learn a little about God's love and grace, and you'll be reminded that you were created on purpose, for a purpose.

I AM Standing Up
True Confessions of a Total Freak of Nature
Luke Lang
RETAIL $9.99
ISBN 978-0-310-28325-6

With all the demands in your life, it's easy to sometimes feel small, worried, or weak, or even struggle with feeling unforgivable, tempted, or worthless. In this book, you'll discover that you're not alone (and you're perfectly normal!), and you'll also find your true identity in the God who created you.

You Are Not Alone
Seeing Your Struggles Through the Eyes of God
Shirley Perich
RETAIL $9.99
ISBN 978-0-310-28532-8

Everyone has secrets, but you don't have to live with your pain all alone. *Secret Survivors* tells the compelling, true stories of people who've lived through painful secrets. As you read stories about rape, addiction, cutting, abuse, abortion, and more, you'll find the strength to share your own story and start healing, and you may even discover how to help a friend in pain.

Secret Survivors
Real-Life Stories to Give You Hope for Healing
Jen Howver & Megan Hutchinson
RETAIL $12.99
ISBN 978-0-310-28322-5

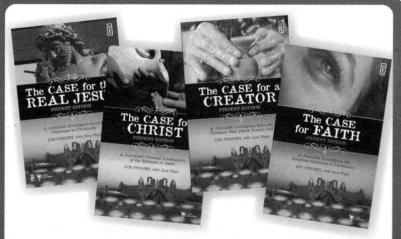

Adapted from Lee Strobel's best-selling books, The Case For...
books for students will take them along on his investigations
about Christ, faith, and creation. Students will find answers
and encouragement that will strengthen their faith.

The Case for the Real Jesus—Student Edition
A Journalist Investigates Current Challenges to Christianity
Lee Strobel with Jane Vogel
RETAIL $9.99
ISBN 978-0-310-28323-2

The Case for Christ—Student Edition
A Journalist's Personal Investigation of the Evidence of Jesus
Lee Strobel with Jane Vogel
RETAIL $9.99
ISBN 978-0-310-23484-5

The Case for a Creator—Student Edition
A Journalist Investigates Scientific Evidence That Points Toward God
Lee Strobel with Jane Vogel
RETAIL $9.99
ISBN 978-0-310-24977-1

The Case for Faith—Student Edition
A Journalist Investigates the Toughest Objections to Christianity
Lee Strobel with Jane Vogel
RETAIL $9.99
ISBN 978-0-310-24188-1

Visit www.planetwisdom.com or your local bookstore.

The Wisdom On... series is designed to help you apply biblical wisdom to your everyday life. You'll find case studies, personal inventories, interactive activities, and helpful insights from the book of Proverbs, which will show you what wise living looks like.

Wisdom On...Friends, Dating, and Relationships
ISBN 978-0-310-27927-3

Wisdom On...Getting Along with Parents
ISBN 978-0-310-27929-7

Wisdom On...Growing in Christ
ISBN 978-0-310-27932-7

Wisdom On...Making Good Decisions
ISBN 978-0-310-27926-6

Wisdom On...Music, Movies, & Television
ISBN 978-0-310-27931-0

Wisdom On...Time & Money
ISBN 978-0-310-27928-0

Mark Matlock
RETAIL $9.99

Visit www.planetwisdom.com or your local bookstore.

Our planet is no longer the paradise God created. In *It's Easy Being Green* you'll learn how to honor God in the choices you make, and you'll begin to understand the impact those choices have on the environment. Sixteen-year-old Emma Sleeth will help you see how you can make a difference at school, around the house, and all over the world.

It's Easy Being Green
One Student's Guide to Serving God and Saving the Planet
Emma Sleeth
RETAIL $12.99
ISBN 978-0-310-27925-9

Visit www.planetwisdom.com or your local bookstore.

Our world is broken, but you can change that. Zach Hunter is a teenage activist, working to end modern-day slavery and other problems facing the world. He believes your generation can be the one to change our world for the better. Inside you'll read stories of real students changing the world and find tangible ideas you can use to be the generation of change.

Generation Change
Roll Up Your Sleeves and Change the World
Zach Hunter
RETAIL $12.99
ISBN 978-0-310-28515-1

Fred D. Lynch III

A HIP-HOP DEVOTIONAL
THROUGH THE BOOK OF JOHN

CD Included

God's Word jumps off the paper and into your heart as you listen to a spoken-word translation of the Gospel of John. *The Script* is a devotional that allows you to listen to the Gospel of John on CD-ROM, then look into your own heart as you spend time interacting with God's Word through creative exercises, as well as prayer and journaling.

The Script
A Hip-Hop Devotional Through the Book of John
Fred D. Lynch III
RETAIL $16.99
ISBN 978-0-310-27806-1

Visit www.planetwisdom.com or your local bookstore.